AF652279

NAGA SOCIETY
Continuity and Change

NAGA SOCIETY

Continuity and Change

Edited by
N. Venuh

Maulana Abul Kalam Azad Institute of Asian Studies

SHIPRA

All rights reserved. No part of this work may be reproduced, stored in a retrieval system or transmitted in any form or by any means, electronic, mechanical, photocopying, recording or otherwise without the prior written permission of the copyright owner and the publishers.
Views expressed are those of the contributors and do not reflect the postion of the Institute.
(2019 PoD Imression, First published 2004)

Rs. 1250; US$ 41.65

ISBN: 978-81-7541-207-1

2024 Impression PoD

Naga Society: Continuity and Change

© Maulana Abul Kalam Azad Institute of Asian Studies, Kolkata

Published by:
SHIPRA PUBLICATIONS
LG 18-19, Pankaj Central Market,
I.P. Ext., Patparganj, Delhi 110092, India
11 47322068; 96500 28065, 9810522367
info@shiprapublication.com
www.shiprapublication.com

Preface

Before the advent of the British to the Naga Hills, the Nagas were in a state of confinement as they followed the traditions of their forefathers in all socio-economic and political aspects. There was hardly any change in society.

The British administration brought about changes in almost all spheres of Naga society. However, in spite of the changes, certain traits of traditional life and culture persisted.

In order to study the problem of change in Naga society, the Department of History and Archaeology, Nagaland University organized a seminar on "Continuity and Change in Naga society" sponsored by Maulana Abul Kalam Azad Institute of Asian Studies, Kolkata under the Ministry of Tourism and Culture, Department of Culture, Government of India. The papers presented at the seminar have been collected and edited into the present book

We are grateful to Prof. J.N. Phukan, former visiting Professor of the Department of History and Archaeology, Nagaland University, for rendering his constant guidance and help in the academic function of the Department. We are thankful to Fr. Dr. Sebastian, Head, Dept. of English, Nagaland University for helping us in proof reading the manuscript. We are also grateful to resource persons, participants who helped us in conducting the seminar successfully.

N. Venuh

Contents

Introduction

The Nagas belong to multi ethnic group and subgroups with varied languages and dialects, cultures and customs and traditions and legends. However, there is similarity in physical features and affinity in culture and their habitats are contiguous.

The seminar "Continuity and Change in Naga Society" brought many scholars to share their views on the scenario of social change that is taking place in the Naga society today.

Shri A.K. Ray speaks of change as the law of life leading to a way of life and a way of thought; both influencing each other in promoting change. Forces of change manifest themselves in the situation in life affecting the way of life and thought, vice versa.

In "Change and Continuity: The Ao Naga village organisation" Ms. J. Lonkumer explores the various aspects of the Ao Nagas from their origin to present day social changes that are taking place. The essay takes the reader through the villages systems with its peculiarities of *Arichu* (Male Dormitory), *Tsuki* (Girls Dormitory), Age setting, *Khels* and the like.

Akang Ao comments on "Change and Continuity in Naga Customary Law" considering various aspects of the institution of a village and its administration as well as the laws governing day-to-day life in the village.

In "Culture Change among the Nagas: Festivals and Dress"

Dr. Anungla Aier looks into the dynamics of culture change among the Nagas with special reference to festivals, dress and transformation that took place when Christianity was introduced. However, the basic cultural framework of the Naga Society has not been drastically changed.

Prof. Lanunungsang discusses in his article "The Working System of Ariju in Traditional Ao Society: A Socio-Cultural Institution", various aspects of *Ariju* (Dormitory) System from its origin to its present day existence. The discussion takes one to the physical structure of *Ariju*, Age group system, objectives and restrictions besides the life and activities in the system.

Dr. S.Victor Babu making his comments on the "Belief and Practices: A Perspective Change", refers to the old tribal beliefs and practices and their transformation with the coming of Christianity. Some practices underwent a radical change, however, most beliefs continue with some modifications.

Dr. N. Venuh analyses "Change of Political Institution of Naga Society" with its traditional tribal forms which was adopted by the British to suit their need and to maintain relationship with the Nagas.

In "Changes in Naga Work Culture", D.Koulie speaks of traditional tasks performed in the Tenyimia community. He also refers to the various traditional occupations of the members of a household.

In "Forces and factors of change in Naga Society" Kekhrie Yhome presents a critique of European metaphysics as well as the problems of homogenizing the Nagas.

Charles Chasie in his "Forces and factors of Change in Naga Society" takes the reader to reflect on some facts about the Nagas and goes into a discussion about the various forces and factors of change both administrative and social. He calls for a sense of history and draws attention to interpret history despite the many limitations.

Aküm Longchari scrutinizes the culture of continuity and change that is inspired by the forces of worldview which guides patterns of human interaction and human relationship with man, nature and the supernatural in the essay "Continuity and Change: World View and Transformation".

1

Change : The Law of Life

A.K. Ray

There is a profound cultural crisis brewing among the Naga people. The rapid spread of Christianity during the past six decades or so together with the post–World War II modernity and now consumeration has erupted into the private precincts of traditional beliefs, mores, ethics and cultural values, and is consequently causing cleavages and conflicts even within families. The fear of the loss of the Naga cultural heritage looms large. As a reaction to this, there is a move among the educated elite to search for the 'roots' of the Naga being; for, they feel that the loss of the 'roots' will result in the extinction of the Naga identity. It is not a revivalist movement, but a turmoil and a churning, akin to what happened to Bengal and the Bengalis, and produced what is called the Bengal Renaissance in the 19th century.

Our seminar will address this historical process of change in its multifarious implications for Naga society. While we must wait to hear what the distinguished scholars and participants here will say, may I, with your permission, restrict myself to the phenomenon of change with occasional references to parallel experiences in another part of our country in another time, which is still working itself out.

Change is the law of life, a cliché but not a meaningless one. All human societies have, since the beginning, functioned on two planes, that of the way of life, and that of the way of thought, and throughout, one has influenced the other. A change in one has invariably promoted a change in the other. One concerns the business of living, and the other the thinking behind the organisation of community existence, its system of values, and its relationship with external forces beyond its control. All this had rationality, which was perfectly valid in the view of the society concerned.

Forces of change manifest themselves generally in the *Sitz im Leben*, *i.e.*, the situation in life. They may affect the way of life, and thus also the way of thought, or the other way about. A telling example is that of the Jews, led by Joshua, settling in Canaan after the exodus from Egypt. "In the process of learning the arts of cultivation from Canaanites, the Israelites were naturally influenced by the fertility cults and other rituals of their neighbours and instructors." It illustrated "the psycho-sociological rule that masses tend to be more concerned with immediate temporal benefits than with future rewards...it was but natural, therefore, that numerous Jews of those times adopted the worship of Baal and Ashotoreth (Astarte), respectively the deities of the yield of the soil and increase in livestock." Some began to worship both Yahweh and Baal, allocating the world of belief to the former and mundane felicity to the latter. Yet others practiced a kind of syncretism transferring to Yahweh all the titles, attributes and modes of worship of the Canaanite gods and goddesses. Thus the determining factor was the *Sitz im Leben.*

It can, therefore, be postulated that autonomous societies, isolated and insulated from the rest of the world, may continue in their traditional ways, but, once that seclusion is breached by alien forces, there ensues a challenge and a conflict with unpredictable consequences. The dimension of this confrontation is determined by the evolutionary hiatus between the opposing forces and so is the outcome. The battle is fought in the human mind.

Societies, which fail to rise to such challenge generally, tend to perish through loss of identity. Those, which challenge the challenge, conquer it and turn it to their advantage, enter a new phase of existence more in tune with its heritage and contemporary circumstances, and thus continue to evolve with a resurgent character. This never means the total abandonment of traditional values, which form the core of the being of a society: they are simply reshaped to fit the new environment and given a new content, and thus they are revitalized. Beginning with the explosive encounter with European civilisation and culture in the late 70s of the 18th century, Bengal and Bengalis had gone through a profound social, intellectual and cultural turmoil for nearly a hundred years. Its product was, what was later described as Bengal Renaissance which laid the foundation for a modernised India, cherishing and proud of its heritage while ever ready to imbibe the best of what was changing times could offer.

The parallel with Bengal begins with the advent of British political power in Nagaland in the early years of the 19th century, but the way the future unfolded itself was not exactly the same. By 1773, British power, exercised through the East India Company, and seen in the person of Warren Hasting, the Governor General, was firmly established in Bengal. That was the beginning of the officially sponsored process of encouraging "native" learning as well as westernised education in English. The patronage given to British Orientalists through the founding of the Asiatic Society brought the Bengalis into contact with a new type of foreigner, the flag-bearer of the intellectual heritage of European Enlightenment. The result was a triggering of a cultural chain-reaction. The point to note is that the East India Company refused to encourage British Protestant Evangelists.

The Bengalis at that time were not as insulted and isolated from the rest of the world as the Naga society was during the pre-British days. Some of them knew enough English to learn about the revolt of the 13 colonies in North America and the French Revolution; clipper ships flying the new US flag were regularly calling at Kolkata port; before the end of the 18th century, the first US Honorary Consul, a Bengali commission agent, had been appointed at Kolkata; and, in any case, interaction with the Britishers since the days of Job Charnock had familiarised them with the foreigners, their ways, their preferences and peccadilloes. The collision with Christianity began after two English Baptist Missionaries, Carey and Marshman set up a mission at Serampore in late 18th century, and two British Presbyterians, Alexander Duff and Charles Grant started their Evangelical work through an educational facility at Kolkata. Their kind of Christianity did not prosper but what it provoked among the Hindus was a powerful intellectual movement to refashion the Hindu way of life and thought.

In Nagaland, American Baptist Missionaries started their work by the middle of the 19th century. The British were against encouraging British Missionaries. They had been badly singed by their experience of the hostility of the local population in the southern part of India provoked by the intemperate activities of the protestant missionaries. Thus they were quite content to leave the task of spreading the gospel to the Americans.

This task was aimed at bringing salvation to the heathen by converting them to Christianity. That needed teaching the Bible, particularly the New Testament, with maximum emphasis on Christ Ministry and his martyrdom on the cross. This far Christianity posed no problem to the tribal mind, conflict came with posing Christian dogma against the tribal belief-system.

At the tribal stage, the life of an individual is an integrated whole. It is a continuous unfolding of wonder; its terminal points are birth and death, and the stages of the interval are marked by what Arnold Van Gennep called *rites de passage i.e.* transitional rites. Sowing the seeds and gathering the harvest constitute together a paradigm of human life itself. Every such society had its codes of ethic and morality; tradition defined the relationship between individuals, that between the individuals and the community, that between the community and its head, the position and status of women and the relationship between them and men, and so on. All this was related in one way or another with the belief systems and worship at the core of which were the mundane hopes and aspirations of the human being. There was a bond, sacralised by tradition, between the individual and whom he or she worshipped. All this made up a way of life not necessarily identical for every tribe.

When Christianity arrived in Nagaland, it sought to sweep all this away at one stroke, and replace it with something that was entirely foreign to the Naga people. Christ's message of love and compassion was understandable, but concepts like God, creation, sin, salvation, immortality etc. were not. What was of immediate value was the setting up of schools and provision of medical care that the missionaries brought in. It is the schools and the introduction of English language, which became the heritage of a revolution that slowly but inexorably unfolded in Nagaland.

This new language became the channel through which flowed in an increased awareness of the vast world of men and ideas outside. As in the case of Bengal in the late 18th and 19th centuries, it is the new ideas, which created not only the desire but also the need to question many of the things handed down by the past. Again, as in the case of Bengal, some went overboard and completely disconnected themselves from the heritage; some tried a compromise while some others sought refashioning. With the advent of the electronic media, there has been an avalanche of new notions, new norms, new values and new mores. Meanwhile, thousands of Naga young men and women had gone outside Nagaland for higher education. They could not but be influenced by what they learned, saw and experienced in the process. All this led to doubts and questioning. The whole of the traditional way of life, its social structure, its belief-systems, its ethic and mores began to be shaken. An increasing number of people began to face the tormenting question whether or not wholly to jettison the past while some decided to plunge headlong into the new wave.

Even the church was not immune from the winds of change and no longer remained confined to the limits set by the doctrine of *Justificatio sola fide,* and by Luther's insistence on observing the prohibitions implicit in the doctrine of "two realms"; it had to find answers to the new perplexities generated by the increasing complexities of modern life. It could not remain aloof from social concerns without facing rejection by its own flock. In the US, as a measure of defence against the onslaught of liberal and modernist tendencies even among the Protestant clergy, various Protestant denominations together adopted what came to be known as the Five Points of Fundamentalism. That was in the late 1920s; by 1930, the movement lost its drive because it lost the battle against the critical and scientific temperament of the times. Eventually, liberal Baptists like William Newton Clarke dropped fundamentalism and adopted a rational stand.

The result of all this is that Naga society appears to stand today at a fork in its history. Social change is a historical necessity for survival. The question is which direction it has to take, and what goal it will aim at. The answer is not always a matter of conscious choice; for circumstances do become the determining factor at times. What is required is the formation of a will. One hopes that just as the Hindus of Bengal had found somewhere deep within themselves the strength and the resilience to tame the forces of change to serve its own good, the Naga society will also stride into the future with a new confidence and pride in itself.

2

The Ao Village Organisation

Origin to Present Day

J. Lonkumer

The Ao Nagas inhabit the district of Mokokchung and comprises of six ranges namely: Japukong, Changkikiong, Asetkong, Lanpangkong, Tsurangkong and Onpangkong.

The Ao Nagas

The Ao nagas believe that they emerged from Lungterok (six stones) lying at the top of a spur on the right bank of the Dikhu just opposite of Mokokchung. The stones are located at Chungliyimti, the first Ao village, which is at present located in the Sangtam are a in Tuensang district. Chungliyimti is considered the seat of Ao civilisation. According to legend Tongpok and his sister Lendina emerged first and they were called the Pongener clan. Then emerged Longpok with his sister Yongmenala and they were called the Longkumer clan. Lastly, Longjakrep with his sister Elongshe emerged and they were called the Jamir clan. Thus three distinct clan emerged who could intermarry; for the Aos follow the rules of clan exogamy very strictly. As per the seniority of the clan certain privileges are given, as in meat shares and the right to wear certain ornaments and ceremonial dress.

Aos are called Aor, which means 'those who went away'. This is in direct reference to the migration of the people from the first village established by the Aos called Chungliyimti. Legend has it that the present day Aos migrated from the original village, crossing the river and dispersing to the various villages where they are living today. The term was coined by those who stayed back, distinguishing the migrants as 'those who went away' (across the river).

The Ao Nagas have two distinct dialects Chungli and Mongsen. The Chungli dialect has now become the standard Ao dialect due to the fact that, the first American missionaries settled in a Chungli-speaking village, and naturally that dialect was learnt and adopted for all subsequent communication and translation. On the other hand, all the folk songs and traditions are preserved and transmitted through the Mongsen dialect.

The Aos consider Chungliyimti to be the seat of their civilisation and it is from here that its history can be traced but beyond Chungliyimti it is obscure. Tradition claims that it was here that the village organisation that is prevalent to this day was initiated and formulated. Both the Chungli and Mongsen system of village organisation originate from Chungliyimti. The institution of Putu Menden (Chungli), Samen Menchen (Mongsen) or the village government was established here and all the conditions and rules of this body were also laid down here, which was handed down to each successive generation through oral tradition, as also the 'Arichu' system (dormitory system). By the time the general migration of the Aos began, the tradition that began at Chungliyimti was already bred in a well defined, well articulated culture and thus the people carried with them the tradition and culture that originated from Chungliyimti to their new settlements.[1]

The Ao Village

To the Aos, family, clan and village affiliations are of paramount importance. The village lands and boundaries are zealously guarded and any encroachment or disputes related to land is strictly dealt with. The land system among the Aos has its origin in the foundation of the village. The common or village lands are the sites such as grounds for dancing and sports, house site for the Arichu (dormitory/morung) building, log drum house, graveyard and etc. and the adjoining forests. The clan lands are those divided among the founding clans near the village while the individual lands are those further away from the village. The founding clans and families settled in the best sites and were allotted the sites depending on the roles they played in the founding of the village. Forest lands in the adjoining areas were taken for *jhumming*, collection of wood for building materials or fuel and other domestic uses etc. by the respective clans and ownership was determined by acts such as taking of forests produce and marking of land boundaries using rivers, ridges, rocks, trees, mound and other natural forms such as these. Villagers who have no land of their own (usually those from smaller clans or those who migrated to the village at a much later date) are given village lands by the village administration for cultivation, collection of wood for fuel, building and other domestic uses. Land is sacred for the Aos and it is widely believed that those who encroach or steal from other's land are cursed for generations. Hunting and fishing is permitted in the village lands to all the villagers, and there are no restrictions with regard to the ownership of land. For example in the clan lands and its enclosed rivers and streams all the villagers can hunt and fish regardless of which clan they belong to.

For the Aos their village is the most important part of their lives. It is from the village that the Aos get their identity and from where they can trace their roots. The feeling of solidarity is very strong among the Aos for their particular villages and as W.C. Smith observed, "intense love for the ancestral village site seems to be characteristic of the people, which keep the villages from breaking up easily"[2].

Tajen Ao asserts that "An Ao village is a highly organised unit in which every man of the village renders his service for his village. He thinks much of the welfare of his village, takes part in the government of the village, works and helps to run it and fight and defends for it. He contributes and subscribes for the service of his village"[3].

Village Council

In the traditional village government Village Council consisting of representatives from all the clans in the village is democratically selected by consensus. The Village Council carries out its duties on the customary laws that were laid down at Chungliyimti. To the Aos, village and clan affiliations are of paramount importance. The traditional village government namely the Putu Menden (Chungli) or Samen Menchen (Mongsen) represented by all the clans in the village exercises administrative and judicial authority within the village jurisdiction. A.W. Davis in 1891 observed that "Each village among the Aos is a small republic and each man is as good as his neighbour, indeed, it would be hard to find anywhere else more thorough democratic communities. Headmen (Tatar) do exist, but their authority is very small"[4] .

Arichu (Male Dormitory) System

The Arichu was a traditional learning academy where boys who had reached adolescence, were required to join the Arichu or dormitories and sleep there. In each village, there were a number of Arichu depending on the size of the village. In a village, there were normally two Arichu, one in each khel. However, if the village was very big there were more than two Arichu established along clan lines. Each Arichu was independent and autonomous. In the Arichu, the young boys were taught the manly arts and handicrafts. They were indoctrinated with the history of the village and the clans and the relations in hostile surroundings. The Aos practiced head hunting and it was in the Arichu that the art of warfare was learnt. The boys were also taught the correct forms of address in an assembly and the right way of narrating stories, singing songs and ballads. All these were taught so that the boys in their turn would become good teachers and leaders when their time came.

The Arichu were strictly taboo for women and no women could enter it. The dormitory system was done away by the missionaries who did not understand its relevance and significance for the Ao villagers.

Tsuki (Girls Dormitory) System

For adolescent girls too, the villagers maintained similar dormitories where girls learnt handicrafts, social etiquette, and all the different songs and chant used in the various religious and social festivals of the village. In some villages, the different clans maintained these dormitories where they sent their clan-women for such education. An unmarried woman of the clan supervised these dormitories. It was in the Tsuki that boys could come and be entertained by the girls and it was here that courtship took place. This type of dormitory has also been done away with.

The Age Set

In the Zunga (Chungli)/Yanga (Mongsen) or the age—set, boys

and girls who have attained a certain age are eligible to join the age—set. Boys and girls who belong to a set where the age difference is 3 years (the age difference may differ from village to village) are considered to belong to one age set. Once a person is in an age set, he/she remains in the same age set progressively till he/she dies. Thus a person gets promoted to the next age set with the same every time the new members join the lowest rank. Each age set has specific duties allocated and the people of that age set perform these duties whenever the need arises. The duties specific to each set remain the same so as each age set gets promoted, there is no confusion as to their duties in the next age set. The age set is extremely regimented and provides the basis for socialisation and for social control. The number of each age-set group differs from village to village. However, the Ao society being patriarchal the age-set for the males is more organised and given more importance. With the induction into the age-set groups Ao male becomes a permanent member of the *Senso*, which roughly translated means citizenship. The specific duties and division of labour in the Zunga/Yanga system also play an important role in the administrative functioning of the village and in maintaining law and order in the village. Thus the Zunga/ Yanga is central to the cultural, political, social and economic organisation of the Ao village.

Village Mephus (Khels)

The villages are usually divided into mephus (Khel) the yimbang (upper) and yimlang (lower) mephus. And each khel has its governing body made up of clan representatives who are assigned certain jobs according to their clan and the position they occupy in the village organisation. Sometimes in a village there may be two linguistic groups with each group living in their respective khels. Each group will have their organisation, for example, in the Chongli khel, the village administration is run by the Tatar Menden and the Mongsen khel by the Samen Menchen. However when certain tasks involving the whole village crop up, the upper and lower khel or the Chongli and the Mongsen khels combine together and work in cooperation without upsetting their individual organisations. The village organisation is based along more or less democratic lines where cooperation is the fundamental feature. In this way the village is based on this age-old system. James Phillip Mills, who served as the Sub Divisional Officer at the Sub Divisional Headquarters at Mokokchung from 1917 to 1924 wrote in his book *The Ao Nagas*, "as with all Nagas the real political unit of the tribe is the village. For most purposes however, the social unit is the 'khel"[5].

Change and Continuity

The social structure is subject to incessant change and the process of social change is responsive to many types of changes. The physical, biological, cultural and the technological factors have been generally regarded as the potential factors of social change. Anything that regularly organised groups of people do or think while living their collective lives constitutes a social system. Any change in such a system, as long as it is repetitive rather than simply limited to a few episodes, constitutes social change. Such a definition does not distinguish between major and minor changes, and it is more interesting to do this by understanding how and why the most critical changes have occurred, as well as the ones which are likely to take place in the future[6].

With reference to the Ao Naga society, W.C. Smith, the American sociologist and missionary wrote in his book *The Ao Naga Tribe of Assam* (1926) that, "The Ao Nagas, as well as the other Naga tribes, made very few changes during their long residence in these hills. Their non-migratory ways and their headhunting habits kept them insulated from all outside influences until very recently,"[7] and that "for a considerable length of time the Ao Nagas, as well as the other Naga tribes were isolated in the hills where unmolested, they went through their narrow round of life, which practically knew no variation from generation to generation"[8].

However with the incorporation of the Ao territory into the Naga Hills District and establishment of a sub-division in Mokokchung in 1889 contacts with the British brought about changes which were "partly accomplished by force, as in the case of political control with all of its implication, partly by suggestion and imitation, due to the influence of commerce, the British government, education and the introduction of Christianity"[9].

The British policy of administration was practical, geared towards securing their colonial interests. For better administration and for the extension of political influence the British built a number of roads linking all outlaying areas with the administrative headquarters. The British also took necessary measures to stop the practice of headhunting, slavery and slave child infanticide. The introduction of a uniform administration code, suppression of certain practices such as headhunting, female infanticide, slave trade etc. development of road communications, introduction of education and Christianity, changes in agricultural processes and promotion of public health and significant influences in bringing about changes in the Naga society in general.

Although the British colonial rule took certain measures to restrict and modify certain native cultural practices, it did not have a direct role in bringing about socio-cultural changes. To refer to Dr. Piketo Sema "the real agencies which brought about considerable socio-political changes were indirect agencies which functioned under the explicit protection of the Government. Of these, the most powerful were Christianity and education"[10].

Christianity was first introduced to the Naga Hills when Godhula, an Assamese Christian, made the initial spadework by learning the local dialect and establishing friendship and contacts with the Ao Nagas. In this way he facilitated the passage for Rev. E.W. Clark the American Baptist missionary whereby he could enter the Ao territory of Deka Haimung village (Molungkimong) in 1876 with the permission of the British government. From Molungkimong Rev. Clark then established a new village at Molung in 1877 and relocated there with some Christian converts and it was from here that Christianity spread to the Ao and other Naga areas. In order to teach the Gospel, education was imparted and thus Christianity and education became the agencies through which immense changes took place not only among the Ao tribe but also all the Naga tribes.

The combined forces of political and administrative control, Christianity, and education brought about rapid changes into the Ao Naga society. But it was the Christian missionaries who were in direct contact with the people and this contact accelerated the pace of change. With conversion and education, the Ao people began to give up their social and cultural practices such as living in the Arichu or dormitories, giving the feasts of merit and observances of 'genna' or taboos. Smith in analyzing the changes brought about the new religion wrote, "Christianity has weakened their taboos and their system of social control"[11]. In the olden days the traditional belief system was accepted whole heartedly and adhered to without any questions and this tended to keep the people under control, for the fear of serious calamity befalling them was very real and very great. As they shed their traditional ways and took to the ways of the

Europeans such as in dress and food habits and the usage of money as the form of exchange instead of the barter system, and the opportunity of working for the Europeans for salaries, the process of change among the Aos began at a rapid pace.

Hutton in the book *The Angami Nagas* (1969) with reference to the changes among the Aos and Lothas wrote "Old beliefs and customs are dying, the old traditions are being forgotten, the number of Christians or quasi-Christians, is steadily increasing and the spirit of change is invading and pervading every aspect of village life"[12].

In their pursuit of introducing the new religion (Christianity) to the "heathens" the missionaries not only changed the lives of the people in terms of religion but also changed their social organisation and social life. The discrediting of rooted beliefs and habits of traditional forms and the bringing about of new re-alignments brought about changes. Education and opportunities for working for the British administration also led to the formation of an educated middle class far removed from the villagers. Through the ages the Aos have assimilated and adapted to new ways and made progress and have been pioneers in various fields. But not all the changes were beneficial. The abolishment of the Arichu system is one such example.

With the decline of the Arichu system which was the most important part of village life, much of the customs, folklore and art and artifacts and architecture of the Aos have been lost forever. For it was in the Arichu that such aspects of Ao culture were embedded. The discipline and orderliness particularly among the young deteriorated and a vacuum was thus created in the village social organisation. The Oral Tradition, which was the form of transmitting the cultural heritage especially of poetry, songs, legends, history etc. of the education. The indigenous knowledge system of the flora and fauna and medicinal herbs has also been lost in the passage of time.

However despite the various changes that were introduced and imposed and the manner in which the Aos adopted and incorporated them into their lives, the fundamental system that has governed the Aos villages since their inception at Chungliyimti survived and remained firmly rooted in the psyche of the people. The parameters of the system may have been altered and with them the systemic principles but the stability and permanence of the fundamental traditional village organisation has endured the tests of time.

The continuity of the traditions in the Ao village organisation is evident although with certain changes first in the governance and administrative system of the village. The Village Council comprising of representatives from all the clans of the village along with the Gaon Buras still administer according to the customary laws.

The age-set grouping is still a important factor for it is only with the induction into the age-set grouping that an Ao male is considered as a full fledged member of the *Senso*. *Senso* may be roughly translated as citizenship. The importance of the *Senso* to an Ao male can be gauged by the fact that the ultimate punishment for him would be the expulsion from the *Senso*, which might as well be a death penalty. The village community work and other administrative functions are divided and allocated according to the age-set grading even today.

The land system in the villages are still based on the traditional system whereby the village, clan, and individual lands are clearly demarcated and the use/disposition/allocation of it is according to the customary laws. Agriculture is still the mainstay of the Ao villagers.

Customary Laws are still followed and fines, taxes or "*saru*" and rules and regulations regarding water, land and personal rights/disputes etc. are based on customary laws, executed at the clan and the village council levels. The inheritance of property is also followed as per the customary laws.

The Clan and kinship system regulates social behaviour to a large extent. Clan exogamy is strictly followed and till today clans are the chief principle units for land ownerships, for mutual support and defense, and the principle links for the whole society are based on kinship.

Thus the Ao village organisation is one whereby the individuals and society are organised into an ordered entity that helps in better productivity and regulation of human behaviour, which minimizes conflict and interests between individual and community goals.

In the context of the Ao Naga tribe, the village organisation is based on the age – set grading, which has clear cut divisions of labour, the clan system and the village council which provides the leadership, and the customary laws which ensures that the code of conduct is adhered to.

Raymond Firth has defined the term "Social organisation" as "the systematic ordering of the social relations by acts of choice and decision." In this view, social organisation is the dynamic phase of social structure, "the continuity principle of society[13]."

The village organisation in the Ao villages is mainly directed towards governance where administration of civic rule and the maintenance of social order are primarily based on traditional customary laws and its associated penal codes. The rules and regulations that govern individual and group behaviour are exercised through a legitimate authority (such as the village council) recognised and accepted by the people. The Ao society like most tribal societies are governed by primordial, interpersonal, kinship and territorial relations, and their organisation as a village is based in these relations, which are cooperative and interdependent.

Conclusion

When Nagaland attained statehood, certain privileges were given to the people with the promulgation of the Special Provision under article 371A where the traditional indigenous culture, law, politics, religion and social life of the Naga are protected under the Indian Constitution. This meant that the Naga way of life as the people had known for ages carried on undisturbed.

However the Ao villages have undergone immense changes in modern times. The lifestyle of the villagers have been transformed with the introduction of modern education and the provision of concomitant modern infrastructure such as electricity, water supply, exposure of print and electronic media, which have influenced mindsets and attitudes, dress codes, behaviour, languages, etc. especially among the younger generation. The architecture of the houses is also giving way to more modern styles with RCC buildings becoming the norm. Development of road and transport networks has made life easier for the villages have buses and those close to the towns even have taxi services. The easy access by road to the markets has made a major impact in the village economy for the villagers can bring their produce to the markets for sale. Though agriculture is still the main occupation of the villagers there are other sources of income such as small grocery and pan shops in the villages while some educated villagers are employed usually in the public sector such as the Government

Primary schools and other Departments such as PWD, Electrical Department, etc.

The attainment of statehood brought in a new form of government through democratic elections, and the electoral system has had a major impact on village polity, sometimes upsetting the balance of power in the village.

The Village Council was recognised and empowered by the State Government and promulgated through the Nagaland Village, Area and Regional Councils Act, 1970. Although the Act has laid down certain rules and regulations for the Village Council to act upon, the customary laws are executed in most of the cases provided it does not contravene or is at variance with the ordinary Criminal Law. Thus the Village Council looks after the executive, judicial and administrative functions of the village. The appointment of a Village Council Chairman is also a new development arising out of this Act.

The Village Development Board, which is a community based programme launched in 1980 by the government of Nagaland, has been the synthesis of the modern and the traditional, whereby developmental schemes are carried out by the Government agency within the framework of the traditional Village Council and the VDB Secretaries (nominated from within the village) are utilised for village developmental works which are organised and executed by the traditional age-set groups and the Village Councils for the community work. Thus the villagers work in tandem with the government for their own development following the age-old traditional division of work.

The benefits accrued from the changes brought by modern technological factors have made the life of the villagers easier in every aspect and the villagers have become more mobile. But the fundamental ethos and characteristics of the Ao villages have remained the same throughout. The Clan distinctions are inalienable, marriage based on clan exogamy is the permanent norm, the village government at grass root levels still continues in the traditional way and the traditional land holding norms are still valid. Above all, the entity called *Senso* is the most important aspect of Ao social life, in both rural as well as urban set-ups, as this defines an Ao's identity. Despite the tremendous developmental changes, the villages remain the most important entity in the lives of the Aos.

REFERENCES

1. Ao, Temsula, 1999, *The Ao-Naga Oral Tradition*, Bhasha Publication, Baroda, pp.10.
2. Smith, W.C., 2002, *The Ao Naga Tribe of Assam*, (Photographically reproduced) Mittal Publications, New Delhi, p. 27.
3. Ao, Tajen, 1980, *The Ao Naga Customary Laws*, Mokokchung, Aowati Imchen, p.89.
4. Elwin, Verrier, 1961, *The Nagas in the 19th Century*, Oxford University Press, London, (A.W. Davis in the *Census of India* 1891, Assam Vol.1, pp. 241-45.
5. Mills, J.P., 1973, *The Ao Nagas*, Oxford University Press, Bombay, p.176.
6. Rouledge and Kaegen Paul, 1985, *The Social Science Encyclopaedia*, London, p.761.
7. Smith, W.C., *op cit.* p.178.
8 *Ibid*, p. 179.
9. *Ibid*, p. 214.
10. Sema, Dr. Piketo, 1992, *British Policy and Administration in Nagaland 1881-1947*, Scholar Publishing House, New Delhi, p. 67.
11. Smith, W.C., *op cit.* p. 190.
12. Hutton, J.H., 1969, *The Angami Nagas*, Oxford University Press, Bombay, pp. vii (Preface)
13. Firth, Raymond, 1951, *Elements of Social Organisation*, Tavistok Publication, pp. 17.

3

Change and Continuity in Naga Customary Law

Akang Ao

Custom is what depicts the inherent way of its people through their uniform and consistent practice of life-style, tradition, eating habit, organisation of social life, religious rites, and matrimonial alliances since time immemorial.

The virtue and quality of the people is known and expressed by their custom and usage *ab initio*. Westlake defines custom as that line of conduct which the society has consented to regard as obligatory and thereby accord the sanction of society as law having binding force upon the State. "Custom is to Society what Law is to State." The role played by custom even today is not insignificant and much of the statute law itself is subject to well-recognised custom to the contrary. For any settlement of dispute, be it civil or criminal, at times customary practice and rule override the enacted law and vice versa. Custom thus, eventually is incorporated as law in the parlance of legislation of any State. Conforming to the above fact, most of the international law too had its sources and concept derived from the customary practices of the Egyptians, Greeks, Romans, Jews, Chinese, and Hindus.

The historical development of civilisation and their custom and law across the world varies from region to region and from group to group. In fact, the difference and variation is as wide as the geographical areas.

Nagas as an ethnic group and a people settled down and occupying the country where they are now, like any other people of the olden age, though they had possessed a compact territory of their own, most of the Naga tribals were isolated from one another and inaccessible owing to deep and dark forests and inhospitable terrain. However, it has been confirmed now that their customary practices specially in the aspect of formation of villages, dispersal of land, social and cultural life, food habit, dresses, matrimonial alliance, engagement of war, settlement of dispute, treaty making and form of worship were by and large same with minor variation from the remote past till date.

The studies of the Naga customary practices leading to the customary law as such, without much enactment by legislatures is a field where social anthropologists and historians ponder with new findings and amusement. There are legends and fables still around all the tribes.

Institution of Village

"Village" to Naga is epic and ionic especially during the remote old days. No village was set up without obtaining clearance of the soothsayer and priest for its everlasting success and prosperity. It was customary to line up and to raise a requisite combination of people belonging to different clans to organize and to form the new village. Naturally, the first parties who settled enjoyed the highest priority of rights and privileges over the others in the allotment of land both for house sites and for cultivation purpose. In the mater of dignity and other prides of social practices too, the first settlers walk over the rest from occultism prostration.

The Naga village enjoys the characteristics of sovereignty equated with the Greek "City State" which was a dominion of its own in complete form of parliamentary democracy. Naga village is permanent although some of them practice shifting *jhum* cultivation.

The primary duties of every village is to maintain the internal harmony of its inhabitants and to work to attain their self-sufficiency. The other outlook of the village is to promote peaceful and friendly relationship with all the neighbouring villages so as to be free from raids and strained feeling from outside.

Administration of Village through Village Council

There is in one form or an other, Village Elder Council that rule the village across the Naga country. In certain areas the Council is represented from the clans whereas in some region it is represented from the khels or by men of merit and wisdom having juristic view. The Elder (known as *Tatar*) Council is undoubtedly respected and known as "Supreme People's Court". All social, religious and political matters are mooted and decided by the Council in conformity with the collective equivocal consent of the village maintaining stoicism. There is no uniform size of the Council members but it represents at best all the segments of the clan or khel in all fairness. As regards the tenure of the council, there are two systems of procedures practiced in the matter of retirement from the council, one form of tenure is 30 years of office when all the members collectively took over the office of the council and relinquished it together on completion of the term of power/ office thus taken over by the group of the next generation. The other system of holding office is retirement from office severely (one by one) on attaining a particular age-group by set tradition by attaining the age of 75 years. The council members served the village without any remuneration whatsoever except certain perks. The Elder Council is the ruling body of the village as 'Curtis Regis' was to the Normans and 'Judices' to the Greek. The council has the justice delivery system within the parameters of customary practices. Generally, all the serious claims, accusations, disputes under both civil and criminal case are tried by the Elder Council. In the matter of judicial power, the council has both original and review jurisdiction in the matter of proceeding on adjudication. The council can take up trial on the basis of complaint or by *suo-motu* or as *De Novo*.

The member of the Council may be removed if he commits any offence or is guilty of misconduct involving moral turpitude. With the pace of time and the formation of the State legislature, the Nagaland Village Council Act, 1979 has been passed reaffirming the erstwhile traditional Council providing all norms of modern concept of law.

Panel Provisions of the Village Council

1. Whoever commits the offence of theft will be liable to compensate the owner by payment of fine, a pig or a cow. The compensation for stolen property is to the tune of seven times the value of property or money according to some tribal customs and no fine is imposed.
2. Whoever allegedly charges another person of theft and fails to prove, the charger shall pay the damage to the latter or fine appropriately for defaming another person. Among some tribes, the aggrieved one shall claim seven counts of the value of the alleged stolen property from the wronged one.
3. Whoever is found responsible for causing and breaking out fire, burning the houses, *jhum* field and woodland

will be fined. The amount of fine varies from tribe to tribe. Certain tribes raise the fine to the tune of Rs. 10, 000/-

4. Whoever destroys some one else's property or kills domestic animals will be liable to compensate on payment of the equivalent to the amount of loss or payment or fined a pig or a cow. Under this count some tribes stake the claim of restoring the destroyed property to seven times the value of the property from the wrong doer, failing which he will be subjected to expulsion from the village for seven years.
5. Whoever intentionally spreads the wild rumour and false propaganda thereby causing serious alarm and panic to the other members of the village will be warned seriously or, be fined a sum of Rs. 100.
6. Whoever buys any property known to be stolen or purchased from a person suspected to be a thief will lose the property. When it is taken away by the rightful owner, he shall be fined Rs. 500 or a pig. No fine is imposed on the person after he loses the property so purchased.
7. Whoever commits the offence of war with any other village he shall be fined a pig or he should face the wrath of the enemy village for his fault. According to some tribe, the offender is only to confess his fault and beg pardon; and no fine or other punitive action is taken in that event.
8. Whoever commits murder shall require to pay heavy fine and also be banished from the village. Among some tribes, in lieu of fine, his house is destroyed and he is expelled from the village for a period of seven years.
9. If any person commits adultery and divorces his wife,

he will be liable to construct a new house for his wife and is fined seven pigs.

10. Whoever trespasses any place of village and conducts himself in a state of intoxication or otherwise acts indecently in such a manner so as to cause annoyance or threat to any person or disturbs the social harmony shall be beaten and punished with a fine of Rs. 50 or above.
11. Whoever claims and contests falsely the rights and title of the founding forefathers of the village, to which he does not belong to, shall be imposed a fine of a pig or cow. The Village Council receives the fine.

Institution of Morung

The 'Morung' was to the Nagas what the 'Hebrew University is to the Jews'. It was a unique institution practiced by many Naga tribes, while some other tribes used other forum or platform in lieu as a learning institution. Morung is where all the young male members of the village conscripted themselves as members up to a certain age-group to train and educate in all round customary practices and life-style and to be groomed to a standard human being to the fitness of the contemporary generation. Morung also served as incessant 'Watch Tower' to detect the incoming enemy's raid and for other village security. The safety and prestige of the village were in the vigilance of Morung. All male members of the village were trained in all disciplines. The old glory and good job done in the past is attributed to the institution of Morung life.

Warfare *vis-à-vis* Head Hunting

Though loss of life and property has been valued as very dear, conflict and warfare could not be avoided as a measure for security and defense world over so also to the Nagas. If any neighbouring village attacked the other without any substantial reason or provocation associated with taking the lives of innocent person or inflicting grievous injuries it was considered sufficient ground for retaliation. However, proper explanation shall be called upon and due reparation as deemed proper shall be claimed failing which the defaulter faced the repercussion. In the process inter-village tribe feud ensued culminating in warfare and killing each other. While the age-old practice of warfare was on, it was natural on the part of the combative groups to contest each other in their valour and skill of warfare by the number of person killed and the number of enemy head brought over to the village. In a world of that age, the status and skills of a person were highly honoured as 'brave and warrior'. Accordingly, the popular term "Head hunting' had been associated synonymously with the Naga warrior who partakes in the warfare.

Killing a fellow human being with or without intention save accidental is tantamount to first degree offence of murder to the Naga custom thereby appropriate punishment was imposed since ancient days as it is with the civilised term of the law. As such, killing does not precede head-hunting, but the general practice was to recover the head if killed to prove and substantiate the fact before the society and prove the skills and valour of the person as a good-fighter. Thus the term head-hunting seems to have been misconstrued in the outside world that the Nagas had simply practiced the head-hunting sportingly. It is time that the term and concept is dismissed once and for all.

Marriage

Marriage is a voluntary union of one man and one woman with the exclusion of any other person. Naga marriage too is strictly exogamous and monogamous as well.

The Naga tribes believe in love marriage. Arranged marriage too is not prohibited either as such by the custom. There is also practice of polygamy with the Angh of Konyak and with the Village Chiefs of Sumi tribes. During the Pre-Christian era, a few other tribes also practiced polygamy in rare occasions depending on the individuals, but it was not as a matter of custom as such. The practice of polygamy is being discharged slowly even by the Anghs and Chiefs as many other irrelevant customs die with the pace of time for good. The exogamous matrimonial custom is also supported by local belief that sibling born of inter-clan and inter-tribal marriages are far superior to the other. Any person indulging in unlawful union and contacting into void marriage such as conceiving child before living together as couple is considered as man of lewd character.

Forming family life between persons within the same party or clan shall be banished from the village or else punished with heavy fine. If the couple is Christian, they shall also be ex-communicated from the church they belong to. As a custom, male proposes to the female and in the event of acceptance, the consent of the parents and relatives of both parties is obtained for confirmation of the marriage.

The practicing marriageable age since time immemorial in the absence of written law is 20 years or above for the boy and for girls 18 years of age. Thus, there is no prescribed age as such, but by depending on the age-group, as calculated by their convention and precedence in the village maturity is fixed. There are three kinds of marriages among the Nagas namely:

(*i*) Valid marriage,

(*ii*) Voidable marriage, and

(*iii*) Void marriage.

Divorce

Like any other civilised society, the Nagas have varied binding grounds for divorce since days till date. However cases of divorce were more common in the past for want of strong social binding and respect for obligation than they occur now.

Grounds for Dissolution of Marriage

1. Pregnancy by another man, which is detected after marriage.
2. Adultery by either part.
3. Unsound in mind and body and suffering from incurable disease.
4. Impotence and barrenness of the husband and wife respectively.
5. Ill-treatment and desertion.
6. For want of children.
7. Conversion of religion.

Re-marriage of a Widower

A man whose wife has died can marry another woman generally after the lapse of three years. A man who divorces his wife is not free to marry another till full alimony as prescribed by the customary measures is made or the divorced wife is remarried to another. On the death of either spouse, remarriage has no bar after lapse of one to three years as the case may be by depending upon the individual. The re-marriage held between a widower and a widow is far from constraints and is simple.

Legal Status of a Widow

A widow is exempted from certain customary and social village subscriptions and practices. Half of the annual household collection is levied on a widow. In all other customary social work of the village like the repairing of Morung, church, *panchayat*, school building and fencing of the village, women are exempted from their attendance, which is compulsory for men folk. However, during annual terracing and repairs of path to cultivation field, widow or unmarried who are living in separate house is liable to contribute tea and edibles to the work place as token of their participation. A divorced wife living in a separate house is exempted from payment of any levy and contribution of the year. A male who has attained the age of maturity for customary and social works of the village and been living in a separate house or with his widowed mother will be liable to work, levy and participate in all village duties and obligations.

Food Habit of the Naga People

Rice is the staple food of the Nagas. Seemingly as a result Nagas are well-built and energetic and strong. Since time immemorial Nagas are a hard working people presumably because of adequate human power having potential force in view of food habit.

There are many delicacies and dishes of the Naga equating the number of tribes. Every Naga relish all kinds of vegetables, meat and fishes.

Dress, Apparel and Costume

The dress and customs of the Naga people are very colourful and exquisite in their respective motives and design. Irrespective of male and female dresses, apparel and customs various patterns of motives and design run through their full length from head to foot. The motives and design certainly indicate and signify the social and cultural status of the wearer in society, which speaks for itself. Of the custom, male armlet and headgear are expensively decorated with ivory, tiger and wild boar tooth, hornbill feathers which are fixed are very significant and meaningful. The other custom blended with goat's hair and cowry shell are also not less meaningful. The shawl and skirts with intricate pattern of motives and design is so appealing and can indicate the group and tribe of the wearer.

Religious Rites

Prior to Christianisation, Nagas believed and worshipped in supernatural and omnipotent gods in various forms. They worshipped the supernatural spirit all round the season and all through festive occasions by rendering deities to appease the god for returns of bountiful blessing and success. Side by side they had also observed numbers of *genna* in the form of worship to intercept and drive away all evil spirits and to invoke good fortune and prosperity. Occasions such as when a new site has to be taken possession or to be cultivated, or seeds to be sown or on the eve of harvest or when a new child is to be born or when domesticated animal is to give birth the deities are worshipped or genna is practiced for good. At every and on change of season and national or social festivals they also offer prayer with a sacrifice of a dog or cock or an egg to the deities. Whenever a death occurs a very serious genna is followed as a mark of respect to the departed soul. They also offer deities a form of worship in every important spot including village gate to prevent the enemy attack and to alter the natural calamity.

Change of Scenario

It is fortunate that Christianity came first to Naga country than the

British-India administration. Christianity came at the height of animism. The force of the gospel is so strong that the incessant effort of the missionary won over the minds of the few Nagas and a great change took place. Before long, after the arrival of Christianity the British-India succeeded to enter the Naga country and slowly but steadily set aside the practice of head-hunting.

With the cessation of the warfare among villages and tribes other practices of the classical period became irrelevant such as Morung life, and other forms were of worship done away one by one opening the new horizon to the Naga civilisation yielding to new life and hope. With the influence of Christianity, the urge for education had been perceived and people rushed towards this end from the beginning of twentieth century. By then Nagas had been exposed to the outside world and could see the other side of the world. A great awareness took place when both the missionaries and British-India agencies worked closely for the advancement of Christianity, education and all round development.

Intoxicated with the new lease and atmosphere of life, free from fear of warfare people realised the fruits of new religion, education, and administration and began to discard the irrelevant old practices.

However, as the saying goes "Old habits die hard" large majority of the customary practice still persist even in the absence of codification till date. As a matter of fact, some of the Naga customary laws have been strengthened and protected by enacting laws such as (a) Rules for Administration of Justice and Police in Naga Hills District Act, 1937, (b) Setting up of Dobashi's Court and Tribal Court (c) Nine points Agreement with His Excellency the Governor of Assam and NNC 1946 (d) Article 371A of the Constitution of India (e) 16-points memorandum of 1960 (f) The Nagaland Jhum Act, 1970 and (g) The Nagaland Village Council Act, 1979.

4

Cultural Change Among the Nagas

Festivals and Dress

Anungla Aier

Culture change is the conceptual formulation that refers to the many ways in which societies change. Hoebel states that culture changes by accretion of inventions and the modifications or replacement of old ways. Culture thus changes and grows by accepting new ways devised by members of its own society or through diffusion and borrowing. Culture change therefore may be endogenous or exogenous in origin and the study, if the process of culture change refers to the actual social mechanism by which the change takes place.

The evidence of culture change in human society is overwhelming. Archaeological findings have demonstrated how change consistently marks the remains of human habitations throughout history. The fact of change is also documented by available historic accounts. This applies not only to data on the past of advanced and developed society but is equally true where the evidence permits a glimpse at the lifestyles of present day indigenous and ethnic cultures.

The need and the importance of understanding the processes and the problems of social and cultural change is revealed by the vast accumulation of scholastic works where different thinkers have viewed the problem from different and contrasting frames of reference. Robert Redfield in his study of the Mexican communities employed the concepts of little and great traditions to analyse the cultural processes of social change. Singh employing the same concept to study the modernisation of Indian traditions reiterated that changes in the culture follow through the interaction between the two traditions in the orthogenetic or heterogenetic processes of cultural change and growth. It assumes that all civilisations start from a primary or orthogenetic level of cultural organisation, and in course of time, are diversified not only through internal growth but more importantly through contacts with other civilisations (Singh: 1973:13). On similar lines, Milton Singer (1964) observed that in the Indian context, the little and great traditions not only interact but are also absorbed interdependent, and the modernizing forces are not only accepted but are also absorbed by the traditional way of life. He conclusively observed that while modernizing influences are undoubtedly changing many aspects of Indian society and culture, they have not destroyed its basic structure and pattern. On the contrary it has given new alternatives to combine aspects of their traditional culture with innovative choices. Singer's concluding observations appear to be quite a relevant and fitting assessment of the direction of culture change among the Nagas as well.

An attempt is being made in this paper to look into the dynamics of culture change among the Nagas with particular reference to festivals, dress and ornaments. The focus of this topic apparently gains significance as one of the most obvious indicators of culture change. Before author embarks on this endeavour, a reference is made to Herskovits (1954) who stated that 'cultural change can not be studied as an isolated phenomenon for change by itself is meaningless until it is projected against a baseline of human behaviour of a given time and nature. Above all it must be contrasted to the phenomenon that is always opposed to it, the phenomenon of cultural stability'. He further pointed out that reinterpretations mark all aspects of cultural change. It is the process by which old meanings are ascribed to new elements or by which new values change the cultural significance of old forms. Reinterpretations can thus be also understood as the retention of old forms with new meanings. With this understanding, the intent of this paper is to assess the forms of changes in some of the important dimensions of festivals, dress and ornaments. In order to undertake a discussion on changes and to better understand the present, it is necessary to dwell briefly on the general outline of some important traditional aspects of the Naga festivals, dress and ornaments.

Festivals

The Nagas are traditionally an agricultural people. All their major religious rituals, ceremonies and festivals focused on and revolved around the agricultural calendars. Each agricultural stage was preceded and followed by one or the other ritual and ceremonies which were performed either by the individual household or by the community as a whole. All such ceremonies can be categorised under:

(*i*) *Private ceremonies:* Among the private ceremonies the most important ceremony is what is normally termed as the Feast of Merit. The feasts of merit can be seen as a mechanism that works both for the community as well as the individual host who bears all the expenses of providing food and drinks to the whole village or villages whatever the case may be. On the one hand the community is given the opportunity to share the wealth of the individual host. In return the material wealth of the feast giver is translated into increased social status and influence in society.

(*ii*) *Public Ceremonies:* Among the public ceremonies, the most important ones are the sowing ceremony, harvest ceremony, and the accompanying festive celebration. Such festivals were punctuated with numerous rituals and genna either for invoking blessings on their sowed crops or by way of thanksgiving for the harvested crops and to purify themselves to start eating the new rice. The ritual observations were followed by a general celebration.

Dress and Ornaments

The Nagas are a colourful people with a creative sense of colour combinations, graphic designs. The various motifs of the traditional clothing are drawn primarily from their everyday environs as well as their ritual life. The use of cowry shells in their dresses is one of the distinctive features of the Naga dress and ornaments. Most importantly, for the Nagas dress and ornaments are more than a matter of aesthetic and decency but the symbolism of it plays very significant role in their culture and social life. They make unspoken clear statements that define the identity of the wearer, their social status, and the group to which they belong.

Changes in Festivals, Dress and Ornaments

The material content of the contemporary Naga society has changed tremendously. Though technologically and economically the Naga society is far behind the rest of the country, the same cannot be said regarding their social living. I may hazard to state that the Naga people are keeping their pace with the tempo of social changes taking place around them by adapting the mode of their social living and culture. And one of the most conspicuous indicators of the changes taking place can be seen in the form of changes in their festivals, mode of dress and ornaments. With this understanding, a brief glance at the various changes is undertaken as follows:

Festivals

Following the conversion to a new religion, considerable changes in the ritual life as well as in the focus of their various festivals took place. Some of the notable areas of transformation are discussed under (i) Ritual transformation, and (ii) Change in focus.

(i) Ritual Transformation

The change in religion initiated structural transformations in their social and ritual lives in order to accommodate Christian ideologies. This transformational process is clearly seen in the context of the Morung, which was not just a social center of learning but also a ritual center. All public ceremonies during the sowing and harvest festivals were performed in the Morung *aphu** (altar) constructed specifically for the purpose in the Morung compound. As Christianity began to grow in popularity, the importance of the Morung as the ritual center decreased. The Christian Nagas began to develop an aversion towards the Morung considering it as the devil's altar. Gradually the building itself fell into disrepair until the whole institution became a thing of the past. In many villages, church buildings were symbolically erected in places where the Morung was located. Gradually and steadily, the church replaced the Morung as the social and ritual center of the community. Another ritual transformation is seen in conducting all important public and private ceremony

* Aphu= is in the Ao Naga dialect.

according to Christian rites while the traditional ritual priests lost their importance.

It is interesting to observe that despite the drastic religious shift and the apparent changes in their ritual life, each Naga tribe has retained its traditionalistic character displayed through the traditional festivals. However, certain notable changes are apparent some of which may be mentioned as follows:

(a) Though the celebratory elements of the festivals are retained, the sacrificial rites and period of *genna* sequence are replaced by organised Christian prayers and the modern order of sequencing the events. Even the non-Christians are more liberal in performing the necessary rituals prescribed by tradition.

(b) While those ceremonies with less communal significance were rejected, important public festivals that enthuse community feelings have been retained and are being revived to renew and reaffirm their ethnic solidarity.

(c) The ritual transformations from group specific to a more general Christian mode also created greater ritual uniformity among the various Naga ethnic groups thereby making room for them to close their ranks.

(ii) Changing Focus

Side by side with the ritual changes, the focus of the festivals has also changed. Traditionally the primary focus of the ceremonies and the festivals ranged from invoking blessings, offering thanksgiving, and ritual cleansing etc. revolving around the agricultural phases. In the contemporary Naga society, the focus of the festivals have widened quite radically. Today one of the most obvious changes is seen in the fact that the main focus of the festivals has shifted from agro base to community base. As I have mentioned above, only the more important festivals are being observed today by all the Naga groups during which their traditional history and folk practices are recounted and traditional attires displayed. Playing of traditional games; singing of folk songs; and folk dances forms an essential component of such festivals. It is where we see a harmonious blending of traditions and modernity where the component items are traditional while the ritual and order of events are modern. Today the festivals thus perform the vital role of connecting the present with the past while inculcating the spirit of communal solidarity and cooperation to work towards common goals.

While specific Naga groups have kept alive their specific ethnic festivals, it is interesting to note that new festivals are in the process of evolving. One such non-traditional festival is the popular state sponsored Horn-bill festival observed every year in December, the Christian festive month. The development of such non-traditional festivals provides a common cultural platform for all the discrete ethnic groups to express their solidarity with one another as well as their distinctiveness as Nagas. Festivals such as the Horn-bill festival though focuses upon promoting the tourism industry, it also create a reason to revive the songs, and the dances associated with Naga festivals.

Dress and Ornaments

The Naga concept of fashion and their daily wear items have been greatly influenced by the Western way of dressing. Today we find that the Western designer brand names have also become a household name whether they can afford it or not. The growing popularity of the global dress and fashion concept clearly indicates the changes that have taken place in Naga culture of dress and ornament. However, we also find that the traditional dress and ornaments have not been totally abandoned. Despite the popularity of machine – made clothing, designer wear, the traditional dress and ornaments have been well preserved and are still in vogue. In this aspect of Naga material culture, pertinent changes as well as continuity is clearly evident. These are discussed under forms; and symbolism.

(a) Forms

The forms of dress and ornaments consist of the materials used, colour schemes and the motifs. The basic materials used traditionally consisted of barks and locally cultivated cotton. The processing of these materials was tedious, difficult and the end results were coarse yarns. The colours used were also derived mostly from plants. The dyeing procedures were also time-consuming and the colours obtained were very limited. Despite all these limitations, the Nagas were successful in creating richly decorated colourful clothes. One of the most apparent changes that we find today is in the materials used and in the ways in which the motifs are being manipulated and the recreated. Due to the growing access to the global market, the quality and the colours made available have increased tremendously in variety. As a result, the finished product has changed dramatically in quality as well as in variety. The Naga weavers today are experimenting with a wide range of materials and colours by combining and recombining traditional colour schemes. However, traditional motifs such as spear, dao, human head trophies, the variety of animal forms such as the tiger, hornbill, elephant, mithun etc. in male cloths and other motifs seen in female dress have not lost their importance. In fact, not withstanding the changes in the use of colours and motifs in the modernised ethnic clothes, the traditional dress of all the specific ethnic groups have changed very little in terms of the colour schemes and the use of motifs. Colours and the patterns of their combinations, which are group specific, have been preserved. The use of Cowry shells as an important material item of decoration in Naga dresses continues to be a distinctive feature of Naga culture. No doubt this item of material is also being manipulated to create new designs side by side with the traditional ones.

(b) Symbolism

In all cultures symbols are used to impart ideas, or to make certain significant statements. In Naga society the ornaments and the motifs of their dress serve as a symbolic vocabulary that makes unspoken statements with regard to the various identity, status and valour of the wearer ranging from tattoo marks on the body and the dress they wear. The point here is that whether it was the specific tattoo designs or the patterns on their clothes and ornaments such as armlets made of sections of elephant tusks, tiger teeth and boar tusks worn around the neck or common items of ornaments, mostly all symbolised one or the other significant aspect Naga ornaments and motif designs are symbolic. For instance the hornbill feather which is a particularly important ornament for all the Naga groups indicates high status of one sort or the other. This item of ornament worn on the head by men symbolizes their prowess as warriors as well as their economic and social status as the only man who has hosted the feast of merit may wear this ornament. The number of the hornbill feather also indicates the degree of the individual's prowess and economic status. Consequently, an individual with two or more feathers has a definite advantage over someone having only one. In the case of women only the wife or the daughter of a man who has the right to this ornament may wear it. The message here is that for all the Nagas such an ornament has to be earned and simply by displaying, it encourages competition to achieve.

With the modernizing process of the Naga society, there appear notable changes in the significance of the symbolism of their dress and ornaments which are indicative of the changing social and cultural values. In the present Naga society the focus of the symbolism of their dress and ornaments appears to be geared simultaneously towards enhancing their Naga solidarity while at the same time preserving the identity of the constituent ethnic identity. For instance the hornbill and the use of its feathers in the ceremonial head-gear minus the values and the symbolic meaning formerly attached to it is now taken as a marker of the Naga cultural identity. Another example can also be drawn from the projection of the Morung and the mithun head as the features of Nagaism. This is evident from the representative creations of the Morung structure and the mithun in the modern ethnic wears and other items of utility. Parallel to this, the symbolism of the specific tribal motifs and ornaments have also been modified in similar ways, whereby inter-village differences are played down and specific motifs are selected by general accord as representative symbols of their tribal identity.

Conclusion

Contact with Western culture and values and the contemporary Indian society side by side with the acceptance of Christian values have initiated the process of social and cultural change among the Nagas. The development of the modern state order, social and economic development initiatives through education and various development packages and the globalizing factors of the modern society have greatly impacted upon the material culture of the Naga society. The contemporary Naga society in appearance thus presents a highly westernised culture. There is no doubt that materially, technologically and in various areas of their social life the Naga people are going through a historical phase of change and transformation where the old is replaced by the new. However, when the external layers of their modern culture is peeled off, we find that the cultural framework of their society have not been changed drastically as commonly assumed. However, what strikes us is that the cultural values and forms have been reinterpreted to meet the emerging situations and needs. Greater access to market facility, economic opportunities etc. have greatly influenced the innovative adaptation of traditional designs and motifs to meet the growing market demands. Today we find increasing varieties of Naga designs; this however has not displaced the traditional specific motifs and designs. The symbolism on their dress and ornaments still serves the function of self and group identification, though the focus has shifted considerably. In the area of festivals also similar trends of change and continuation is visible. Though the ritual aspect of the festivals has been changed drastically as a consequence of Christianisation, this particular fact has created greater ritual uniformity among the ethnic groups. In the festivals we also find the innovative reinterpretation of the perspectives where the celebration of traditional festivals provides a platform for the members to express their history, achievements and to urge one another to exploit higher status of honour. In conclusion it is stated that though tremendous transformations have taken place in the past hundred years or so, yet the core of the Naga society and culture have not changed much.

REFERENCES

1. Herskovits, J. Melville, 1955, *Cultural Anthropology*, Oxford Publishing Co. Pvt. Ltd.
2. Singh, Yogendra, 1973, *Modernisation of Indian Traditions*, Thomson Press (India), Faridabad.
3. Singer, Milton (ed), 1959, *Traditional India: Structure and Change*, Philadelphia.

5

Working System of Ariju in Traditional Ao Society

A Socio-cultural Institution

Lanunungsangs

The Ariju, popularly known as 'dormitory' or 'bachelors' house' (morung in Assamese) is one of the most significant social institutions found among the tribal societies of the world in different forms. This institution is the fundamental basis of the Naga cultural heritage. In fact, it is one of the oldest and strongest means of social control. As a unique institution, it serves as the agent of social security with trained and disciplined personnel. It could be explained better in terms of a modern 'University or military headquarters' because of its functions, nature of training and propagation of ideas. However, it is neither simply a night shelter for bachelors nor a mere assembly of young boys of the village. It is certainly a boys' school and a perfect learning institution. It can be said that there was no formal learning institution in Naga society before the coming of modern schools and colleges. Hence, it occupies a unique place of learning center in Naga society. It is a place exclusively for men only. Ariju in Ao term is not only a sleeping place for bachelors but it serves the needs of society such as social security, promotion of culture and master craftsmanship. It is in fact a real training institution that promotes the process of socialisation of people in general and men folk in particular. Indeed, all the boys after attaining the age of 12-14 years sleep there until marriage. This is one of the best examples of rural social institutions from where socialisation of a man takes place.

Literally, Ariju refers to 'fortress' from where the approach of enemy is carefully watched. '*Arr*' means, the enemies and '*Ju*' means to guard or watch. Therefore, Ariju means, 'watch people of enemy' in the real sense of the term. Precisely speaking, 'Arr-salang' that refers to "the enemies' fortress" is the antonym of Ariju. Therefore, Ariju can also be considered as 'Security Hall', and an open 'Trench System' in modern term used by military in warfare. J.P. Mills said that, Ariju is a 'Public School'[1].

The Origin of Ariju

One may ask how and when this institution emerged. The oral tradition claims that Ariju is as old as the village, because in olden days Ariju was constructed simultaneously with the establishment of a particular village. It is difficult to trace the exact date or year of the origin of this institution. However, the circumstance of erecting Ariju is clear. It is said that when all the male members were away in their fields, an unknown enemy entered the village and took away all the essential ornaments. This created a sense of insecurity among the villagers and an emergency meeting was held to study the causes and future course of action. They decided to make a Sabang(c), Jobang(m), a platform in an ideal place from where the arrival of enemies could be traced easily. This platform is called 'Arr-jobang', which was transformed into Ariju later on. By and large, *Sabang* was an open roofless platform. Later on, roof was attached over it to protect the village guard

(*Tsütenmonger*) from rain and sun. Gradually, it turned out to be the most decorated house in the village like that of a rich man's or village Chief's house.

In due course of time, it was their understanding to depute one or two warriors as sentry to guard the village from any kind of eventuality. Every day and night, the villagers used to assemble in the *Arr-jobang*[2] to keep vigil against enemies and for safety of the village. This gave them a moral boost and a sense of social security that turned to be a living institution later on. The system of *Tsütemonger* is still practiced in Ao Naga villages today. The duty of *Tsütemonger* is to guard the village the whole day while others are working in the field. It is their duty to call the people working on the field during emergency like sickness, death, fire incident etc. they will also deliver the official letters/messages to the next village received on that day. While on duty, they will keep on moving from one corner to other checking every house in the village to know if there are certain emergency calls needing the help from the *Tsütemonger*. In the evening they will inform the next house/ person to relieve them and to perform the duties of *Tsütemonger* the next day. This will continue through out the year in turn.

In olden days, *Arr-jobang* or *Arr-salang* became the center of attraction, which was located in the center of the village. It was naturally so attractive and beautiful that it commanded respect and honour. As an assembly hall of male folks, it was respected by one and all because of its grandeur. From that day onward, when a new village was founded, the first duty was to select a suitable site for construction of the Ariju. It is clear that this came into existence when the Aos settled at Chungliyimti. In other words, Ariju is as old as the legend of Chungliyimti or Longtorok.

Ariju in Chungliyimti

While establishing a new village, the Aos generally erect the Arijus within a few days just after completion of the construction of individual houses. Accordingly, *Senden-Riju* (a common assembly hall for all clans members) was first constructed. Later on, as the population increased in great numbers, other Arijus were constructed that belonged to different clan members. Ariju was in fact revolutionised while living in Chungliyimti. History tells us that in Chungliyimti, the entire village had two distinct *mepu/khels* namely yimpang (upper khel) and *yimlang* (lower khel). Accordingly, two more Arijus were added namely, *Tongpang-Riju* for upper khel and *Aong-Riju* for lower khel respectively.

It can be stated that two different linguistic groups namely, Chungli and Mongsen inhabited each khel. They met very often at *Senden Riju* for important deliberations. As the population increased, more Arijus were added such as *Lemtu-Riju, Ajen-Riju, Ningdang-Riju, Pemyu-Riju*, and *Chipang-Riju*, occupied by different clans. In course of time, when the Aos dispersed in different directions, they carried the same idea of the Ariju system of Chungliyimti and they constructed this security hall in every village.

The number of Ariju depends on the size of the population of the village. In bigger villages, they make several Ariju or at least two, but smaller villages make even one.

Construction Process

Construction of a new Ariju is a tedious job and it is not a very simple matter because a stringent step-by-step process has to be followed based on strong customs and religious beliefs. First, the site is carefully selected observing *genna* by the village priest. When a new village is established, Ariju has to be constructed immediately after the completion of the construction of the individual houses in the village. During this time, all members of the Ariju are actively engaged in different assigned duties as per the direction of the senior members. Collection of new materials from the jungle and erection of Ariju is fixed in a planned manner. Though it is a difficult job, they take it as a challenge and consider it to be the most joyous occasion. Members would contribute their best architectural genius. It is indeed an occasion of competition not only in terms of physical strength but exhibition of their own creativity in construction of Ariju in every *khel/mepu* in Ao villages.

Construction of a new Ariju is very important within the village circle. As agreed upon, the site is selected after observing rituals performed by the priest or eldest clan member. This is followed by collection of new construction materials. Pigs and cows are kept ready for the purpose of sacrifice and ceremony. On the appointed day, Pongen clan members ceremoniously slaughter the animals. At the same time of sacrificing each animal, the villagers would say, "My sons flourish and grow like cane shoots and banyan trees and become wise in their Ariju"[3] . For this the Pongen clan members who offer the sacrifice would get their share of meat about 1 kilogram. Then he would observe 'genna' for six days. After all the animals are sacrificed, the senior most member of the Ariju digs the pole for the front post and two other members carry the two main posts Tongshijak. These two members should be married persons, however their wives should not be pregnant at that time. Normally, the members of the Ariju are unmarried males. However, he may continue his membership till his term expires along with his age group members.

The carvings on the pole are smeared with the blood of the animals sacrificed by a senior member of the Ariju. Each *zünga* (age group) is assigned to do a part of the construction. For example, Zütsüng and Salang group may make the *sümang* (protecting wall). On the front gable from the top to the door, there is a peculiar decoration called *Tsüma/Süma*, which is made by the Anpa age group. The young boys make all other decorations on the roof. All the essential materials for decoration are supplied by those assigned by the Süngpur age group. Generally, it takes three days to complete the construction, and on the last evening, a grand feast is usually organised in which the members of the Ariju and a few old men, including women participate.

The Onger, in commemoration of the new Ariju, observes three days *genna* and sacrifices a fowl. Singing and dancing around the building continue accompanied by feasting. Then they proceed to the houses of rich men and sing throughout the night, which is called *kimak.* Six days *genna* is observed at the start of construction of the building[4] . It is interesting to note the celebration and ceremony after completion of its construction. The evening becomes more joyful and busy as the Ariju boys engross themselves actively participating in the ceremony. The senior most member known as Onger of the Ariju consecrates the new construction with a cock, beating on its back and plucking its feathers, with a simultaneous pronouncement of words invoking god's protection for the boys from any misfortune and also to bestow upon them honour and glory.

In the process of ritual, the cock's throat would be slit and its blood sprinkled on the posts and walls. Then the entrails are pulled out on which omen is read. Finally, the sacrificed cock is hung at the front carved post. Thereafter, the members participate in drinking rice beer (yi), sharing the blessings. Then, led by the Ariju *Tir*, the group enters the Ariju brandishing their daos and tapping on the walls and post, producing thunderous sounds accompanied by emitting war cries, sustaining the voice as long, loud and clear as possible to be heard by the whole populace in the village. This is a sign, which drives away the evil spirits from the Ariju and invokes prosperity to the village. They then, sing in unison.

The Physical Structure of Ariju

The structure may vary from place to place. However, the nature of its functions and procedures are the same throughout the Ao country. Generally, the Ariju is built near the gate within the village fence. Its size and nature may vary from place to place. However, the typical and standard size is often about 16.60 by 6.60 mts. with a front gable 10 mts. above the ground and the height of the rear is about 5 mts. above the ground level. It always has a platform called Salang, just in front of the Ariju on which the young boys perform many things. Naturally, this house must have both eaves (*kip*) and protecting wall (*tsümang*). The eaves of the thatch roof come down near the ground. The walls are made of solid bamboo pieces, fixed in the ground very close to one another called *tsümang*, tightened with cane ropes in order to escape the sudden spear thrust at night. There are no other side doors or windows in Ariju except two doors in the front and at the rear. There is no passage straight inside the Ariju.

On entering the front door, there is a structure made of bamboo matting fixed with the wooden beams extending from one side of the wall to another. The height of this structure is about five meters to prevent the enemies to cross over it quickly. The main post is at a distance of about two meters from the front door. It is embellished with carvings of Tongshijak, elephants, tigers, snakes, human heads and hornbills. A little beyond this, there are two fireplaces, one near the front door and the other at the rear. The former is meant for the seniors and the latter for junior members. Ariju is generally repaired every six years by its member.

Inside the front entrance is laid the sü-mangkong (resembling a mithun in repose), a barrier consisting of a huge log is laid on the ground across the entrance covered with the most slippery bamboo matting structure. It is too high for an ordinary person to jump over. Any intended attacker who tries to step over it would definitely succumb to it due to the slipperiness that is placed to scramble the enemy. Even if an enemy gets through the door, he has to jump on it and down the side and end up in self-exposure. This is the main blockade, which is placed in front. It is made of hard bamboo mat about five feet in height covering the lower portion except the door. About three decorated bamboo posts are tied at a distance of every six feet making the wall impregnable. The upper portion of the front wall is covered with palm leaves and split bamboo battens. Between the upper portion of the wall and the roof, about one and a half feet space is left for ventilation and that is covered with well-knitted bamboo split. All these fixtures cannot be broken easily at the very entrance, an elaborately wooden carved post with hornbill, tiger, human heads, and snakes stands representing the symbol of heroism.

A typical Ariju may have at least several hearths on the beaten earthen floor and separate partitions. The first chamber is called *Tzüin* (water storage), where water, fuel, wooden bowls, sandstone balls and other materials are kept on one side and the other side is used as a urinal place, the Ariju drum is hung in the middle. The second and the third partitions are reserved exclusively for the seniors and the last one for juniors. In the upper portion of the ceiling, reeds for torches called *kümpok milen* are stored covering the entire space of the ceiling from the front to the back collected by its members during winter months. In most of the Arijus, there are several thousand bundles of each *Kümpok milen* stored for the whole year or more. (One bundle consists of 10-12 pieces about 8-10 feet long).

It is to be mentioned here that an Ariju is incomplete without the presence of a *kümpok milen,* a beating drum inside the hall, and a decorated log drum in its courtyard. There is a fireplace in both the second and the third partition. On both the sides of the partition, rows of planks are kept as cots for each individual. In certain Arijus, bamboo-made common platform is used as cots. Every evening, the boys do their respective jobs near the fireplace. After completion of their works, they would join in singing. Any outsider from another village who has no host or place to sleep in the village is allowed to sleep in the Ariju under the strict surveillance of the boys. An unknown stranger is not allowed to visit the Ariju without the knowledge of Ariju Tir, the Commander.

Age Group System in Ariju

The entire life of Ariju is solely based on the network of age group system, *züngaren. 'Zünga'* means, 'age group,' and '*ren*' means 'in lines'. In fact, without the working system of this, the organisation and its functions would not be possible. The whole picture of an Ariju is demonstrated by different activities undertaken by different age groups *züngaren.*

Züngaren in Ariju may vary from one linguistic group to another. However, the most common to all the groups is that, each *zünga* has to remain on the same status for three years before they are upgraded to a higher status. The membership of Ariju is extended to all the male members irrespective of their status since they are entitled into its system at the age of 12 to 13 years. The oldest *zünga* retires every three-year at about 25 years. Therefore, the tenure of Ariju for a person is about ten to fifteen after which he would automatically become a village councillor in the village administration, *Putu Menden*. A bachelor, above the age of thirty or so, even after his term is over may continue to be a member of the Ariju, but he is exempted from all compulsory contribution of the Ariju. At the same time, if a man marries at the age of twenty-one or so, he ceases to sleep in Ariju, but he is bound to pay all compulsory contributions until his tenure expires along with his age groups[6] . generally, Ariju consists of the following six *zünga*, mainly:

1. *Süngpur,*
2. *Tenapang,*
3. *Zütsüng/Sangremzen,*
4. *Salang,*
5. *Senyim*, and
6. *Jozen* or *Ajozen*.

Each group has a well-defined status and they play their roles accordingly. It is a very distinct classification of age group, which is the foundation of Ariju. In most cases, every age group maintains a two-tier system *i.e.* upper and lower grade within the same cadre. The social structure may vary from place to place but the nature, structure, and their functions are almost the same throughout the Ao villages. Their powers and functions are briefly discussed below as a frame of reference.

Süngpur (c)/*Tzür* (m): 'Süngpur' means, 'wood carrier or server' and the term 'Tzür' stands for 'pouring water'. The day one is registered in *tzüba yanga/zünga*, the first stage of manhood, he parts from his parents and partially stays in the Ariju, to become a member of this institution of learning. This is the junior most age group which goes on upgrading every three years till they become *Jozen* from where they retire.

Below *Süngpur*, there is another preliminary group known as *Tzüi-tatong/Kongshir* (trying to crow) who are eligible to enter the Ariju after three years. However, they are considered as immature. *Süngpur* serves for three years as *tzütar* (water carrier) and ten-year (errand). On the night of induction to Ariju, all the *Süngpur* deposit six bundles of fuel-wood; each measured by the circumferential reaches of their arms length. They also bring six bamboo containers (*tsüshi*) and one wooden bowl. Six of the boys would carry a bundle of fuel-wood about seven feet in diameter. Sufficient water is stored and the hearth would be lit before the arrival of senior members of the Ariju. Some *longshilong* (sandstone balls) are kept burning to be immersed in water. The sole purpose of those balls is to provide warm water instantly to the senior for bathing. Prompt service is given in order to avoid punishment. Since they are under service training, the first three years are spent in manual service to the elders. They are supposed to do all sorts of duties assigned to them by the seniors at any time, such as collecting water, fruits, sharpening the daos, massaging, collecting firewood, making dresses etc. There is no question of saying 'NO' in Ariju system of training. Thus, severe ragging continues for almost three years.

It is a time of genuine test of life, and they are bound to take it as a challenge in life to reach real manhood. They are compelled to slog in all situations. Failure to carry out the orders of the superior may result in severe punishment. These three years period is a time of vigorous training. In fact, one has to cross this stage as a training period in order to bring up a man in good discipline. This is the beginning of socialisation in the Ariju system, which makes him a worthy citizen in the society. The age of entry to the Ariju earns the social status of a man. Hence, every adult male is expected to become the member of this institution as and when he attains the prescribed age.

Tenapang

This is the second category of age group in the Ariju. After the vigorous training period is over, the boys are automatically promoted to this category. Here, there is no severe disciplining; they are bound by all the rules of the Ariju. 'Tenapang' refers to blooming age who is ready to get married. Most members marry at this age and get settled. As the new batch enters, *tzür/züngpur* is promoted to *Tenapang*. They work under the control of their senior *zünga* and they take the charge of the flower garden and green fresh leaves. Their main duty is to teach the younger age group in the Ariju, disciplining them in every aspect of living including war tactics. They are also supposed to do considerable manual work. However, they are not yet free from basic rules and punishments. They are still under heavy duty and do all the above menial works. During the period, they carry food for raiders but are considered too young to take part in head hunting. In this way, every *zünga* is promoted to the next age group till they attain the most respectable age group.

Sütsüng

After a period of three years in *Tenapang*, they are upgraded to *Sütsüng*. This is the middle class group from where they attain the status of seniors. No additional work is assigned to them except some designated work at the time of making a new Ariju and repairing that takes place after six years.

Salang

The fourth category is called *Salang*. After serving in *Sütsüng zünga* for three years, they are upgraded to this *zünga*. Thus they become the senior class by virtue of their status and long experience. They are exempted from hard labour and are free from punishment but bound to abide by a set of rules. In fact, they are the trainers and master artisans. It is their responsibility to train up the juniors in different specialised trades.

Senyim

Senyim is the fifth category of age group. They are now next to the most senior *züngza*. '*Senyim*' refers, the money, '*Sen*' means money, and '*yim*' means, to engage, meaning to engage/ arrange money. They are the chief buyers of animals for feast and ceremonies. They act as the finance section in modern organisation. Without their knowledge nothing is bought, especially the livestock. The *Jozen/Ajozen* seek their advice in times of critical juncture.

Jozen/Ajozen

This is the last category of age group in the Ariju system. They are considered as commanders of the Ariju and its members *Arijuchanger*, the most matured age group. They are the real bachelors of the village, almost free from all rules and disciplines but command respect and honour. The Ariju life retires out from this stage. Most of them leave the Ariju and settle independently. If a man fails to marry even at this stage and wish to remains a member of Ariju, he can do so and remain as *sangremer*, confirmed bachelor. He ceases to sleep in the Ariju but remains connected with *Arijumen/ Arijusanger*. This group is the senior-most age group in the life of the Ariju. They are the overall in-charge of the activities of most age group in the life of Ariju. Everything and anything has to be done under their command. That is why; they can be called as the commanders, administrators, rulers and controllers of the Ariju life. The main duties of this group are building and repairing, maintenance of the Ariju system and its organisation, making decisions in the affairs of the Ariju administration and assignment of duties to the respective *zünga*.

They are the best subordinate body of the village administration and social control measures. They can directly impose fines on culprits and lawbreakers in the village. Any dispute between two *zünga* or more is brought to this body, they give final verdict and their decision binds all the six *zünga.* In ceremonial feasts, they organize the feast and lead in war dance of the village and its welfare. In fact, they are the military force on command; the force to defend the land. They command high respect and honour by virtue of their seniority and qualifications. From this organisation, they are inducted into *Putu Menden.* In every age group, four to six eldest members are selected to lead their group who represent different clans. The authority of their group lies mostly upon them.

Ariju Tir

Over and above, there is a man called *Tir* (Father of Ariju) who is also the religious head. It is a lucrative post. The Arijumen choose him based on his status, wealth, and knowledge of war tactics, heroism in bringing enemy's heads or for his contributions to the life of the Ariju system. Though he may not engage actively in war, all strategies of war are chalked out in his house, which is the headquarters of military exercises, here, the warriors gather to discuss plans and finalise them with his consent. Before going to war, young warriors sleep in his house so that the sex taboo is observed. He performs all religious ceremonies before and after the war. He predicts omens and can postpone war. As a religious father, the *Tir* performs all religious sacrifices and is the incharge of management. He is the war leader and commander, a man of integrity, bravery and source of inspiration to young warriors. He encourages the young warriors, gives them meritorious awards, and also punishes them for all their follies. He helps and supervises the construction of Ariju, supplies all the requisite building materials from his own land.

He may lend paddy for celebration of Moatsü festival and for other unavoidable expenditure. He is the mediator between the village councillors and the *Arijusanger* in time of crises. As a father, he takes the head of every animal that is killed in the Ariju. In return, the *Arijusanger* render assistance to him by working in his field and repairing his house free of cost, and thus he enjoys a prominent place in the village society.

The tenure of a *Tir* is unlimited. One may be a *Tir* during his lifetime. However, an inefficient or incapable *Tir* is replaced. He is also bound to supply a pig or cow every three years to the *Arijusanger*. This is called 'Tir-kümzük', 'return gift'. Non-payment of this gift is regarded as a debt that will be remembered for generations to come.

The working of age group system is an interesting living example of the Naga cultural heritage. There is no caste system in Naga society at all and social stratification of Naga society is mostly based on clan hold, and age group system.

In Ao term, the literal meaning of age group implies a group of people born within a given period of three years inclusive of both male and female. They form a *zünga* that refers to a particular age group. *Zünga/azüng* refers to 'count' in Ao term and therefore, anybody born within a particular period of three years, is counted as the same age group. Thus, every member of that zünga maintains the prestige and identity from his childhood until he dies.

There is a common term in Ao called 'züngapur' and 'züngatsü' or 'purzüngar' which means, 'the same age group.' The persons born within that same period of three years address to each other as 'züngar' to male and 'züngatsür' to female. 'Pur züngar' is a common term addressed to common gender as childhood friend indicating the same status in terms of age being the same age group. Usages of such terms are found to be very sweet and meaningful. In the name of *pur züngar*, they can come closer to each other like the class mates.

Every züngar maintains a distinct demarcation of self identity not only in terms of years but also at the level of social interactions, marriage, exchange of labour, contributions to family lives and societal concern and challenges. They maintain equal social status and command equal respect and honour throughout their lives. In this way, one will notice a strong sense of 'we feeling' among themselves. The degree of intimacy among themselves is found to be higher than their age group in their social life. Aged people count the names of the living ones of their age group with sweet reminiscence. They maintain self-respect and self-pride among themselves. They feel as brothers and sisters whether they live in their village or away as 'züngapur' and 'züngatsür' or 'pur züngar'. The distinctiveness of a given age group is demonstrated more when the boys enter into the Ariju and the girls into the Tsüki at the age of 13 to 15 years, that qualifies them to people hood. From this time, they would no longer sleep with their parents in their house but in the respective established institutions as discussed in this section.

As they enter into these institutions, they are considered as adult members in their society and as such, they are no longer considered as children but responsible citizens in their society as they attain the status of real people hood. From this stage, they are enlisted in all sorts of community work compulsorily. Most of the community works is done according to age group in every village. They know their duties or else the seniors assign the duties as per their established customs.

Each zünga work in the fields of their parent in turn. This is called *yangtep*, a kind of exchange of labour in the fields. In this system, two to ten or even more form a working group, which consist of both girls and boys of the same age group. They work in the respective fields in turn. For instance, they will work in the field of Mr. A one day and the following day in the field of Miss X and so on till everybody gets the facility. They go on rotating in the same way till the major works are completed. This is one of the living examples of labour force in tribal society. The owner of the field may provide the day meal or else they carry wrapped lunch individually. However, curry has to be provided by the owner of the field. The boys sharpen the tools and implements of the girls and the girls carry all minor items from the village to the field. While returning home, they carry firewood that is arranged by the boys generally in advance. This is the time of making friendship, and learning from each other through constant interaction.

Objectives of Ariju

The main objective of Ariju is to defend the village for which, they need to have well-organised trained personnel. In order to achieve this, they have to perform multifarious functions covering a large area of societal needs ranging from social security, civil administration, manpower training, personal development, promotion and preservation of culture etc. in fact, Ariju is the anvil of the Ao cultural heritage.

The main objectives of Ariju are as follows: (a) It is their responsibility to see that the village gates, the fort and the fencing around the village are made so that no enemies can enter their village for raids. This gives the villagers a feeling of safety and security. (b) It is their duty to keep vigil in and around the village to signal any possible intrusion by the enemy and thus guard the village. (c) The principal objective of the Ariju men is to defend their village as trained warriors; they have to be ready to fight the battle. During inter-village wars, all men except the disabled or wounded men engage in the battle. Abstaining from the battle is regarded as the greatest shame on the part of a man. Heavy fine is imposed on those who fail to perform their duty. They are the front liners to defend their village. (d) It is the responsibility of the Ariju to appoint young men, in turns to guard the village gates day and night, called *meitkar*. In modern terms, they perform the similar duties of military force. The village authority, in addition appoints *tsütenmonger nokimonger* who act as the messenger in the village as discussed above. (e) Vigorous training is imparted in the Ariju making the Ariju men, the most disciplined persons not only in day-to-day life but also in the battlefields. The boys of the Ariju serve as the front line defenders in the village raids and act as one of the best voluntary organisations in the village system of administration.

Restrictions in Ariju

As a general principle, no married person is allowed to sleep in the Ariju. After marriage, the members retire from its membership. In addition, no woman can enter into this peculiar institution of young men. Even the courtyard of this house is highly restricted to woman and if she comes near the vicinity, it is regarded as a bad omen. The members of Tsükir cannot come near the Ariju though the members of Ariju normally visit Tsüki. The under aged male members cannot sleep in this house unless he becomes a *bona fide* member of this institution after attaining maturity. Ariju is also restricted to strangers. Age is the determining factor to become a member of Ariju. It is the Ariju system, which maintains the most stringent discipline and code of conduct rules. The Ao system of Ariju is more distinct as it plays multifarious roles based on distinct social structure having definite functions at every stratum.

The Life and Activities in Ariju

The life in Ariju is absolutely a kind of military training, full of activities that lead to perfection of manhood. It has its own set of conduct rules that have to be followed by every Ariju man. No one can remain at ease because it is a training institution more or less-like a public school. It has a *Tir*, a titular head, and highly structured social system under which everybody keeps engaged as teachers and learners. The master artisans are highly qualified in their trade though they do not have academic degrees from Colleges or Universities. They are highly expertise personnel in their own fields and the best trainers in their circle. This denotes Ariju, to the one of the busiest training institutions. The busiest period of the Ariju, are the festivities, village raids and construction and repairing of Ariju and the winter months.

As commented by Christian Missionaries, the institution of Ariju acts like a 'Public School'. A Public School is found very active and busy during daytime and during the night it becomes a deserted place. The life and activities of Ariju is just the *vice-versa*, as the Ariju men would go to their respective fields during the day time. Hardly two or three members as sentry men guard the Ariju when the rest of the members go to work. This institution provides many instructions, which covers the entire aspects of a man's life. The subjects taught in Ariju are many that includes both technical and non-technical. Under technical section, the following are the major subjects:

Defence Subjects

Under this, military war tactics, offensive and defensive methods of war, ambush, village raids, trench making, preparation and handling of war equipments like dao, spear, bow, shield, fire stone rolling and throwing methods, fixing booby traps and spike etc. are taught. They receive extensive training on those items of traditional war tactics. This can be compared with that of the part of military engineering in modern terms.

Housing Subjects

Under this, designing, construction of houses, Ariju, village gate and fencing, wood and bamboo works, masonry and metal works, painting and carving of wood, stone and pottery etc. are taught.

Agriculture and Allied Subjects

Under this subject, various techniques related to cutting and burning jungles for cultivation are minutely learned from the elders. Pest control measures, livestock management and introduction of new variety of seeds and their preservation, techniques of grain storage system, tree plantations etc. are taught.

Industrial Subjects

Under industrial subject, various handicraft techniques are taught which include bamboo and cane works, wood and stone works, tools and implements etc. The senior members of the Ariju teach lessons. Most of the items like baskets, mugs, spoons, dishes, wooden or bamboo bowls, cages, knife, dao, spear, shield, scabbard, smoking pipes, weaving instruments etc. are manufactured in the Ariju mostly in the evening. The master artisans usually teach both theory and practical on these subjects.

Woodcarving is a specialised subject. The Ariju boys learn wood carving works. Each one of them can do it beautifully. They can turn solid log into any kind of object like tigers, hornbill, mithun's head, snakes, lizards, human skull etc. they are talented wood carvers. This makes Ariju almost like an institute of Polytechnic-cum Military Training School for boys in modern terms. They collect enough raw materials during winter months to suffice during summer and autumn. Gradually, all the Ariju men become specialised personnel in every subject. It is interesting to note that many of the senior members would obtain as many work as possible to be done from the girl's parents in order to win favour from her family members. Those who work are then entrusted to the juniors, to be done on their behalf. As a result, Ariju boys are always found actively engaged on various types of works such as making knives, dao handles and spears, weaving instruments, sharpening dao, smoking pipes for girls, basketry works and so on. Workloads are obtained even from Tsüki and its maidens to be done by the Ariju boys. Besides this, many a times, married people also bring various kinds of work. Therefore, in the evening the Ariju boys are effectively engaged in different kinds of works that are not very pleasant to many of them. This is a clear example of exploitation in Ariju system. Techniques of capturing tigers and wild beasts and other wild animals, community fishing, trapping techniques, war and ceremonial dance are all also taught as main components under this section.

Socio-Cultural Subjects

Under these subjects, story telling, folklore, rituals, ceremony, matrimonial relations, family management, art of speech, recitation of poems and songs etc, are taught. All these subjects are generally taught in the evening hours. The Arijumen gather every evening with new stories and experiences to share with their counterparts. The experience of Tsüki and their love stories are narrated with a joy of humour in every corner of the Ariju.

In winter months, the Ariju boys collect enough reeds (*rangsüng/kümpok milen*) from the jungle and after splitting each of them into bundles, they are properly kept in the ceiling of the Ariju. These are used during emergencies as flaming torches to pass information at the time of death, ailment, and festivals and for messengers sent out to other villages at night. These reeds are thoroughly dried owing to regular heat and smoke caused by fire inside the Ariju every evening. Hence, this proves to be an effective tool. If any intruder enters the village, the boys would come out in groups with such torches raising alarm by shouting loudly, "oooooo-heeeee" thrice. The older boys instruct the juniors to beat the drum inside the hall and also the giant log *deum süngkong,* outside the Ariju courtyard. It is normally beated well by 15 to 20 persons at a time, announcing the war signal. The other age group blocks the village gates and the rest go around the village holding the reed torches to locate the enemy. Through this tactic, the intruding enemies are caught or driven away from the vicinity of the village. On such occasions, it is mandatory for each of the Ariju boys to take up the war dao, spear, and shield wherever they move either in individual or in groups. All the Ariju men are required to be ever alert and vigilant to face such an eventuality at any time. Lazy, lethargic and absentees are severely punished and looked down in their society and rated as girls.

Being well trained not only in village raids, but also in hunting wild animals, the boys at the later stage are capable of catching even wild animals alive. They encircle the areas where wild animals hide and go on ringing them beating the bushes with sticks to clear the jungles as they draw closer to the prey making it easier for the older men to advance deeper and closer.

The tigers and wild boars are killed in a ceremonial way with great jubilation. Many animals are hypnotised by the thunderous sound of the Ariju men. The killed tigers are kept on a bamboo rafter and brought to the village with long procession of war cries.

The dead bodies are then kept upon the bamboo platform near the village gate. In all these, the Ariju men take the lead. This is their part of life. No Ariju boy can abstain from such community works like ringing of wild animals, community fishing and village road clearance etc. whenever a rich man performs a feast of merit, they provide fuel, fetch water, husk paddy and supply bundles of reed torches on the night when the mithun is killed. The carcass of the mithun is dragged to the host's house and the Ariju boys watch over it the whole night.

Life in Ariju is not a time of mere training and punishment. It is full of enjoyment, recreation, leisure, and merry makings. The occupants are fully engaged during festivals and ceremonies, which is a part of their life. The Ariju serves for learning songs, love affairs with girls, besides they are taught to make varieties of musical instruments like bamboo flutes, stringed instrument made of hairs, bangles out of bamboo and buffalo horns which are played during festivals. Their visit to the Tsüki, to meet their lovers is a joyful and unforgettable moment that makes their life happier. Songs sung on such moments are still fresh till date. Moatsü is a national festival of the Aos. The cost of this celebration is met by transporting paddy from the field for rich men such as the Ariju Tir and others. From this fund, they purchase a pig or cow for the festival. Despite the difficult situations they encounter especially during the time of training, every Ariju man feels that life in Ariju is the best period of their lives. That is why even after their retirement from its system, most members frequently visit the Ariju.

Nature of Punishment

The nature of punishment in Ariju is very peculiar, characterised by real testing of manhood. The nature and types of punishments are not simple for an ordinary person to bear. The senior age groups impose punishments to the junior groups. The newly registered groups are the people who suffer most under the stern hands of the seniors. Sometimes, they are sent to the most strategic jungles alone at night to pick up certain fruits, flowers and *daos* left behind by the seniors intentionally. They are sent with threatening words that, wild animals or evil spirit would attack them. Other forms of ragging includes tying their hands from behind and forcing them to collect certain articles from behind, pouring cold water when they are asleep, making them jump over burning fire and taking out chunks of fire with teeth from the burning fire. They are also sent out to the jungle without food for several days. They are forced to play the ringing and chasing.

During this period, the slightest mistakes earn them severe punishments. The tasks of juniors are very heavy and difficult, any sign of resentment results more punishments. When the parents of the girlfriends reject the senior Arijumen, the juniors receive mass punishment from the frustrated and angry seniors. Even the partition walls and firewood brought by the boys are piled in the middle and burned. Breaking of wooden bowls, partition walls, burning of entire fuel are indirect punishment for juniors because all these damages have to be replaced the next day by them failing which their punishments are doubled. Therefore, no boy would dare to fail any assigned punishment. The boys are ordered to put reed leaves in their earlobes and light the fire and compelled to go round the fire till the leaves become dry. Sometimes the senior members will send out the boy alone even to haunted places at dead of night. They will order the boy to go to the far distance immediately alone and leave a significant mark there. The seniors will check the mark on the following day.

The mildest punishment is to massage the seniors every night and serve them with their needs. The boy's parents cannot comment on the nature of punishment imposed on their sons. In his way, all the juniors are imposed upon by their seniors as routine matters or else as punishments. These are the nature of ragging in the Ariju.

Downfall of Ariju

Nowadays, the Ariju has lost its importance and usefulness, as its principal objectives were to guard the village against the onslaught of headhunters of the bygone days. Over and above, the spread of Christianity and modern education has contributed in reducing the importance of this institution. It may be mentioned here that the practice of having such bachelor's house had become redundant with the shift from animism to Christianity. As a result, the traditional practices that were once associated with the old religion have now been completely abandoned. Today, it is not possible to have Ariju in its traditional fashion because most of the village boys and girls pursue their higher education outside the villages, mostly residing in hostels. The young boys and girls who do not stay in hostels stay with their parents till they get married.

After the inception of Christianity, churches have attempted to introduce hostels in place of Ariju but failed. Today, only in few villages one will find Ariju as a model. These days, no boys sleep in the Ariju and its activities and functions have been completely changed. No Ariju system exists today in any of the Ao village like before.

Thus, the golden age of Ao civilisation ended with the closure of the Ariju institution. This is the most regrettable aspect of Ao culture and society. The church also failed to organize this institution in the form of Christian hostels at different levels. That is why maximum number of dropout youth occurs in their society today. Many young men and women are found loitering in every village aimlessly. When night comes, they find no proper shelter with proper guardian. During the daytime, they spend most valuable hours doing hardly anything. These are the results of the downfall of Ariju system in their society. Unfortunately, the modern educational system also could not adopt the disciplining system and the methods of imparting education to the youngsters. Otherwise, the method of education in Ariju was excellent especially towards making a total human being. The Ariju was the center of value education. This is a great challenge on the part of modern educational system in contemporary social planning programmes.

REFERENCES

1. Mills, J.P., *The Ao Nagas.*
2. M. Akang, *Ibid*, p.70.
3. Alemchiba, *A Brief Historical Account of Nagaland*,1970.
4. M.Akang, *Ibid*, p. 69.
5. M. Akang, *Ibid*, p.66.

6

Beliefs and Practices

A Perspective Change

S.V. Babu

Every traditional society attempts to explain, predict, and control its environment through religion. Nagas are no exception to this phenomenon. The patterns of beliefs of the early Nagas appear to be animistic. Hemmed in both sides by the massive mountain ranges of the hills and by the very walls of the typical village, most Naga groups developed religious systems which were very locality-specific, that is, highly elaborated with respect to the immediate, localised microcosm in which villagers lived.[1]

The traditional Naga cosmology consisted of two-tiered scheme. At the upper tier was a supreme deity who underpinned the universe and who, though benevolent, was but vaguely understood and seldom approached because of his remoteness from everyday concerns of Naga communities. At the lower tier were a host of minor spirits. Since these spirits were thought to have controlled the specific relations of everyday life—disease, crops, rain, human fertility, death, etc. it was through their agency that these phenomena could be explained and predicted.[2] These spirits were considered malevolent and needed constant appeasement, usually in the form of sacrifice of pigs, fowl or other living things to keep them from harming individuals or whole villages. For these purposes services of village specialists were required.

At one level early Nagas believed in the creator God, who was known by different names to different tribes. The Ao Nagas called this supreme deity *Lungkijingba,* the Semas called it *Alhou,* the Lothas called it *Potso,* the Angamis called it *Ukepenopfu,* a supreme goddess.[3] The existence of creation was ascribed to the work of the creator who was thought to be supreme and beneficent. But this spirit does not interfere in the everyday life of Nagas, although he is in charge of final destiny.

At another level they believed in spirits of the sky (sky Deities). The Aos believed in *Lizaba,* as the creator of the earth and deity in control of the rains and consequently of the food supply for the rice-growing Aos. But *Lizaba* was also malevolent because he commanded sickness and disease. As such Ao villages held annual ceremonies in his honour in June, during which pigs would be sacrificed outside village gates and eaten by the officiating priests.[4] The Semas called these sky spirits *Kungumi.*

At third level they believed in swarms of spirits which inhabited the everyday world of Nagas and were generally harmful. They are everywhere in the village, in the field, in the jungle, by streams, in trees and in the huge boulders.[5] The Aos called them '*tsungrems*', the Semas called them *tughami* and Lothas called them *Nagza.* They are supposed to be malevolent but can be propitiated through sacrifices.

In order to propitiate these malevolent spirits, early Nagas performed a lot of *gennas* or ceremonies. These *gennas* varied from tribe to tribe and from region to region.[6] The word *genna* is used in two ways: (i) it may mean practically a holiday, *i.e.*, a man will say 'my village is doing genna today' by which he means that owing either to the occurrence of a village festival or some such unusual occurrence as an earthquake, eclipse or burning of a village within the sight of his own, his village people are observing a holiday, and (ii) *genna* means anything forbidden.[7]

Closely connected with these beliefs are practices such as head-hunting, human sacrifices etc. This practice of head-hunting was embedded in the belief that the occasional capture of a human head was essential for maintaining the fertility of the crops and well being of the community.[8] Again human sacrifices were offered to ensure a good harvest.[9] The captured people from raids were treated as slaves and slaves sold for economic gains were often sacrificed by their new masters.[10] Among other beliefs, Nagas thought that certain men possess the power of turning themselves into tigers, often known as tiger-men. These tiger-men are still a living legend in Naga society.

Even after the assumption of colonial administration in Naga Hills, the British did nothing directly to disturb the traditional religious beliefs of the people.[11] It was seen to be inexpedient to interfere with Nagger customs and beliefs.[12] But it took necessary measures to remove certain social evils and practices associated with the customs and traditions of Nagas.[13]

It was in this backdrop that Christianity was introduced in Naga Hills. For missionary work and the spread of the gospel, the missionaries undertook various measures. They began to translate gospels into many tribal dialects. While translating Bible, missionaries leaned heavily on Naga cosmological aspects. In the beginning, Ao *Bibile* translated both *kyrios* (Lord, master) and *theos* (god, God) by the Ao word *tsungrem*, a word that denotes simply 'a spirit' not endowed with any specific attributes. It was a generic term not a proper noun.

Again, E.W. Clark used Ao word 'molomi' (great fire) to Bibilical Judgement Day. It was only in 1945 that J.E. Tanquist revised 'tsugrem' with Jihova. In the same way, Christian supreme deity was identified with *Ahou*, the traditional supreme deity of the Semas. This was a decision of considerable importance, for its effect was greatly to facilitate the cognitive transfer from 'old religion' to the 'new'. And by using the Sema supreme deity's name to stand for the Christian supreme deity, as opposed to planting a foreign word into the language, there never really occurred a transfer at all, but only a greater refinement and elaboration of Semas' conception.[14] Tanquist, the missionary to Angami region, translated God as *Ukepenopfu,* the Angami female supreme deity. The missionary did not realize at the time that ending 'pfu' was a feminine ending, although the word Jihova which his friend Stanley Rivenburg used did not become popular. So Tanquist hoped it would be accepted as the equivalent for Christian God.[15]

Once Christianity spread, missionaries began to implement Christian principles strictly. Candidates for baptism were required to know Christian doctrines and furnish evidence that they had not participated in any 'heathen ritual' nor drunk any beer for three months.[16] And even in dress new converts adopted Assamese jacket and body cloth. Later more and more European styles were adopted such as long shirts, mauve coats, khakhi short or white blouses imported from plains.[17] Later this became a controversy between the Missionaries and the Government.

Another central part of Naga culture was morung. This was the lodge, where young men of the same exogamous clan slept before they married and moved into separate houses. It also frequently served as a guard-house and it was generally located near the village gates. And it was the focal point for major village celebrations and feasts that marked its ritual year. The missionaries forbade their male converts to live in the village morung. This institution gradually disappeared from society.

Another basic Naga institution that was discouraged by missionaries, presumably because of its association with Naga deities, was the Feast of Merit. This was a carefully ranked sequence of feasts given by individuals for their village or for their clan within a larger village. The giving of this feast raised the sponsor's position in the eyes of his peers, thereby constituting a major channel of social mobility. Great quantities of food supplies were expended on these Feasts of Merit and they occasioned much drinking and merrymaking. Again, missionaries forbade drinking rice-beer, a drink that was central to the Feasts of Merit and other ceremonies.

Thus while some of the practices underwent a sea-change, most beliefs continued with some modification. Colonial state was not as much instrumental in bringing this change as were Christian missionaries and their activities. Education, too, has its role in contributing to this reformative process in the Naga society.

REFERENCES

1. R.M. Eaton, 1984, 'Conversion to Christianity among the Nagas 1876-1072' in *IESHR*, Vol. 21, p.4.
2. *Ibid.*, p.5.
3. Hokishe Sema, 1986, *Emergence of Nagaland: Socio-economic and Political Transformation and the Future*, Delhi, p. 36.
4. Smith, 1925, *Ao Nagger Tribe of Assam*, London, p.78.
5. Mills, J.P., 1926, *Ao Nagas*, London, p. 217.
6. Hokishe Sema, *Emergence of Nagaland*, p.42.
7. Davis, A.W., 1891, 'Census of India', *Assam*, Vol.1. p. 249.
8. Christoph Von Furer-Haimendorf, 1969, 'Morality and Prestige

among Nagas' in M.C. Pradhan (ed.) *Anthropology an Archaeology: Essays in Commemoration of Verier Elwin*, 1907-64, London, p.156.

9. *Imperial Gazetteer of India*, 1908, Vol. XVII, p.12.
10. Hunter, W.H., 1879, *Statistical Account of Assam*, London, p.181
11. Elwin, Verier, 1961, *Nagaland*, Shillong, p. 78.
12. Haimendorf, C.V., *The Naked Nagas*, p.50.
13. Piketo Sema, *British Policy and Administration in Nagaland, 1881-1947*, Delhi, 1992, p.60.
14. Eaton, R.M., *Conversion to Christianity*, p.38.
15. *Ibid.*, p.41.
16. Rivenburg, 1941, *The Star of the Naga Hills*, Philadelphia, p.117
17. Clark, M., 1907, *A Corner in India*, Philadelphia, p.33.

7

Change of Political Institution of Naga Society

N. Venuh

In the pre-colonial days each Naga tribe occupied its own specified territory, and each tribe was grouped into a number of villages, and each village occupied a well marked area. In course of time, each village emerged independent and had its own administration. The village assembly alone developed as the apex organisation among the Nagas. As J.P. Mills notes "As with all Nagas the real political unit of the tribe is the Village". The village was thus the highest form of organisation among the Nagas that represented political, social and religious bonds.

Each village-state pursued an independent policy. Administration was indigenous and independent.

The Village Chief

The Naga tribes which had chiefs, chieftainship certainly constituted the important element in their polity.

The chieftainship was normally hereditary in most of the Naga tribes but it was not necessary that a son of the chief should always become the chief when a chief died, any able-bodied member of his clan, who had given proof of his capacity and efficiency, could be chosen as the chief after successfully performing religious rites and worships to their God.

The chief was the important element in the polity of the village. The chief was assisted by village councilor who represents *Khel* or Clan. It may, however be noted that the extent of power of the chief varies from tribe to tribe. In some tribes and villages, he was merely a nominated head more in the nature of a ceremonial institution than anything else. But in some other tribes and villages, the chief was very powerful.

Among the Konyaks, the chief known as Angh was highly autocratic. The Angh is the head of the administration and of political affairs. Whatever he says is the law to his people. The Angh was assisted by his Councillors, but the final decision was always taken by the Angh himself. Nobody dared to object or reject his views. He was the authority over his village or the area. The power and position of the chief could be categorised under three types:

(*i*) Democratic,

(*ii*) Semi-autocratic, and

(*iii*) Autocratic.

The important role of the chiefs in Naga village, their status and position in traditional Naga society are an indispensable prelude to understanding the Naga polity.

Village Council

Every village had its own council. It constituted the supreme body of the village. The method of selection of the council defers from tribe to tribe. But normally the eldest of the clan is nominated to represent the village council. The function of the council can be divided into three categories:

(*i*) Executive,

(*ii*) Administrative, and

(*iii*) Judicial.

The village council was the most important political institution in Naga society. Changes took place after Nagas came in contact with British in 1882.

The British adopted a native system of administration which would suit local test and at the same time be conducive to maintaining law and order among the tribes. Accordingly, the age-old traditional form of administration most suited to the peculiar conditions of the Naga people and their society, was reinforced. In pursuance of this policy, the existing institutions based on local customs and traditions were sought to be linked to the European concept of administration by the addition of certain local agencies. However in course of time they gradually eliminated the existing system and estranged the tribal. By the recognition of the traditional leaders and elders, an integration of the existing leadership into the colonial political frame work was tried to be achieved. Under the colonial rule, they introduced three layer system:

(*i*) Gaonburas,

(*ii*) Dobashis (Interpreters), and

(*iii*) District Administration.

At the beginning in 1882, Gaonburas (G.B) were appointed following a traditional practice and the customs of various communities. There is a Head G.B for the entire village and then there are one G.B. and one Assistant G.B. from each Khel or Clan of the village. The Government interest was served best as they were recognised and appointed to assist the colonial administration in the carrying out of their respective village administration. Although the chiefs or headmen were given due recognition as undisputed leaders in their traditional set up, their recognition as village chiefs or headmen was done with the intention of making them loyal agent of the colonial administration at the lower reaches. Thus, while continuing to be the leaders of their people, they became an important link between the British Government and the masses.

The powers and function of the Gaonbura as representative of colonial administration, were determined by the Government. The Gaonbura had no participation in formulating the policies regarding their own affairs. On the other hand, the Gaonbura only received directions and supervision from the district officers.

Another institution that served both as an instrument of pacification on the Naga and as a native team of intermediaries between the rulers and the ruled was that of the Dobashi. This institution was one of the chief means through which the British Government established successful relations with the Naga tribes.

The services of the Dobashis were effectively utilised by the district officer in many ways. They helped and strengthened the district administration to enable him to have free access to the local people in perfect security. In addition to their duty as liaison between the Government and their local people, the Dobashis were at the same time employed as judges in the villages. Dobashis also advised the British officers in the settlement of cases according to the customary laws. The local disputes among the villages, Dobashis were often dispatched for timely intervention and pacification of the villagers.

The third layer or institution of colonial policy was District Officer who supervised overall administration of the Nagas. Even though they did not interfere in internal matters of the tribe directly almost all the policy was framed by them and direction was given to the Gaonburas and Dobashis. These officers were exclusively Europeans.

Thus British Government transformed the political institution of the Nagas into three layer system not directly but indirectly to suit the convenience of the Government and to maintain relationship with the Naga. No doubt before the British colonised the Naga territory, each Naga village was independent, and the village council was the sole authority to frame the policy and maintain law and order of the village. But after British colonised the Nagar it introduced a system which every village had adopted as a common system and administered under the direction of the district officer.

Though the village chiefs and village elders enjoyed supreme authority without interference of any higher authority, it was now demolished.

The power of the village council though apparently retained, was in fact, reduced by restricting its traditional powers to settle all matters of any degree. Dobashi, which did not exist in the village court, now has become legal where matter of any dispute are settled in Dobashi Court.

Even though many customary laws and system of administration were reduced we find that in the villages some traditional systems still in practice.

As regards the Naga political will, formerly it was expressed through the Village Council, and each village had its own will. Now by coming under one central authority which, at the district level, wielded by the Deputy Commissioner, the Nagas are united both politically and territorially.

REFERENCES

1. Venuh, N., *British Colonisation and Restructuring Naga Polity* (Ph.D. Thesis unpublished)
2. Hutton, J.H., 1921, *The Angami Naga*, London, Reprinted by Oxford 1969.
3. Horam, M., 1975, *Naga Polity*, Delhi.
4. For Deptt. Pol. A January 1882 No. 135.

8

Changes in Naga Work Culture

D. Koulie

Work culture of a given society refers to the activities performed by every member of that society to produce economic goods by rendering physical and mental labour, to term as 'culture'

It denotes the continuity of human activities throughout life and follows as a course and means of life from generation to generation. Human life continues in the process of birth, growth and death and passes the tradition to the following generation, so also work culture is a continuous process of human activity in continuity. Traditionally, the Naga work culture is for production of economic goods that are based on basic needs of an individual, the family and the village community. The main occupation of the Nagas is agriculture, animal husbandry and, agro-based industry, weaving, handicraft, pottery, black smithy and trading. Whereas agriculture remains the primary occupation, others are associated or additional work. Within those associated works, pottery, black smithy and trading are very limited. The yearly income of a family is assessed by the annual crops harvested. The wealth of a family is measured on the basis of the annual crop and counting of heads of cattle. The status of a family in the society is elevated by the wealth possessed. Work culture that emerges out of human needs is also the source of traditional education system. The life of a person undergoes various stages of work culture. The learning process goes through practical works and experience and therefore every normal individual can earn to sustain life for survival and be a genuine and responsible person in the society.

Factors and Motivation of Early Social Changes

The trend of change of Naga work culture is more or less owing to the multi-factors of modern civilisation. Like historical transformation of a society all over the world, the primary factor that had changed the Naga society and work culture is the spread of education. The Nagas were the immediate neighbours of Assam and Myanmar, since time immemorial. Our ancestors lived their own way of life and had hardly been influenced by any foreigners till the 19th century. The entry of the British colonial rule in Nagaland followed by the spread of education and Christianity by the American Baptist Missionaries are the two direct influences in transforming the Naga way of life in all aspects. The apparent transition of Naga society seems to have a uniform pattern. However while attempting various sources of traditional work culture and the course of its change, author confines my resources, to Tenyimi community.

Since the inception of Nagas entering into contact with the West, formal education has motivated personal and social outlook towards elevation of personal status, responsibility in society, to gain monetary power and choice of white collared jobs. The exercise of the power of the government through its servants weakened the traditional practices and rules of the villages during the colonial power. Those who were educated, were given official jobs with regular monthly salary. Those persons were considered to have monetary power in the eyes of the general public. They were also considered responsible persons in shaping the future of Naga society. Irrespective of the rank, a government servant was highly honoured by his or her fellow Nagas. The Deputy Commissioner and his immediate subordinate officers were admired like semi-gods. Those exercises had deep-rooted influences on the illiterate masses. As such, the mind of the parents was set to take away their children from traditional work culture for formal education. The mind of the people was also further influenced by the situational circumstances. For instance, the realm of Naga society widened and human needs increased at the embrace of new social outlook. Even in the field of education the need of learning materials increased, the commercial goods from other part of the country, particularly syndicate goods were highly attractive to the native people. Those indigenous household goods Nagas produced without any monetary expenditure, were time consuming products. But the free flow of those machine-made household goods or luxury goods in the market strongly attracted the native people.

Tradition of Work Culture

Before we enter into the nature of work culture, the system of land holding needs to be mentioned as working of the people depends on land possession. Unlike many other Naga tribal communities, Tenyimia community can have (a) Family land property, (b) Clan land property and (c) Village community land property. Most of the joint land properties, other than family land property, are for jhum cultivation. The terrace fields are made from family land. All immovable properties of a family are concentrated on the head of the family, because inheritance law of the ancestral properties is vested on the male line. The self-acquired property, including immovable properties, of course, can be bequeathed to daughters.

Traditionally, the work culture is uniform for all families in a village community. Every individual is the 'jack of all trades' in work culture. One has to acquire all forms of work culture, as the basic needs of every family are the same. The first and foremost duty of all individual is to engage in agriculture to produce food and store it for the year. The main crop is rice. Tenyimia community has three types of cultivation – terrace cultivation, jhum cultivation and gardening. All the three types can be simultaneous cropped. Every family has at least, one or two plots of terrace fields. Maximum harvest of rice is from terrace fields, but engagement of labour is much more in jhum fields. Apart from the paddy cultivation, some types of vegetables on the terrace walls and fruits such as guava, banana, mango, orange etc. are planted around the field. In jhum field, variety of beans, Naga dal, taro, sweet potato, soya bean, yam, ginger, sesame, chillies, tomato, cucumber, millet, *khuvie* (shallot) and some variety of maize are cultivated from those jhum fields. From garden crops such as mustard leaves, garlic, variety of green vegetables, maize, chillies etc. and other common fruits such as guava, banana etc. are grown. Normally, gardens are chosen enclosing a dairy farm. Kitchen gardens are also practiced. To mention the paddy annual harvest, approximately an average family produces about 20-30 bags. These are neatly dressed and brought home to store in storing baskets made of bamboo-rope.

Every family has its moral obligation and duty to produce sufficient foodstuff for the whole year. Poverty may be caused due to natural calamities such as storms, heavy rain, hailstorm etc. in fact, there exists some individual families who were comparatively very poor. However, such condition of a family might be due to exile/migration of the family from the native village or premature death of the couple. The art of Tenyimia agricultural system is a whole year activity. The seasonal work of terrace cultivation and jhum cultivation comes alternately. As such, disguise-employment is never experienced in Tenyimia work culture. The following periodic distribution of work in agricultural practice may be examined from the table:

Table: Tenyimia Work Distribution Culture

Months	*Terrace Cultivation*	*Jhum Cultivation*
January	Tilling of soil	Softening of the tilled-soil.
February	(the same may continue and	Sowing of millet and Burning of the weeds and soft soil.
March	Preparation of nursery beds)	Redistribution of the burned soil and sowing of paddy seeds starts from the 20th March to 10th April.
April	Sowing of paddy seeds on Nursery-bed.	Const. of hut and drainage in the field.
May	Repairing of irrigational channels	Nurturing of young paddy.
June and July	Transplantation of seedling on the Terrace field.	Harvesting of millet crop.
August	Cleaning of weeds	Cleaning of weeds and cutting of grass. New jhum field, guarding the paddy Birds/ animals.
September	—	Burning of field followed by soil tilling.
October	—	Harvesting
November	Harvesting	Harvesting of additional crops.
December	-do-	Redressing of field for millet

Festivals fall in between various types of work. Some works are minor and hence people can have time to attend to other works of different nature.

Animal husbandry, as mentioned earlier, is a major source of income. Every family has a number of cattle, chicken and pig. Rearing of dogs and cats are few. Whereas other animals are kept domestically, cattle is kept in the form of farming. Sheds are constructed at a place chosen by the cowherd or the owner of the cattle. If the cowshed is built at the preference of the owner it is usually built near the terrace field, so that the cow dung can be utilised as manure during cultivation. If it is built elsewhere, the family of the cowherd can make it into garden.

Keeping cattle generates work culture. According to the Tenyimia tradition, every child both boy or girl, rich or poor has to become a cowherd at the age of about 9 or 10 years. They continue to look after the cattle for about 5 years. Some extend this service upto 7 years. In the first year, they look after about 10-20 cattle, depending on the experience of the cowherd. The seniors look after about 50-60. The cattle belonging to a number of families are put together to be looked after by a cowherd. During that period, a cowherd learns how to rear cattles and to provide veterinary attention to the cattle. A cowherd is paid annually at the following measures :

1. Paddy 2 rhajü per head of cattle (1 rhajü is approximately equivalent to 1 tin)
2. Meat 10 pieces of beef and 20 pieces of pork (approx. 1 kg) per head of the cattle.
3. Rice beer About 3 litres of rice-beer per head of cattle.

The cowherd is affectionately treated. In a year, beginning from the first day of the major festival, Terhünyi, which falls in the later part of December, the cattle are set free and the cowherd has winter vacation like students and teachers of today's academic world. This vacation lasts for about 45 days. During this vacation period, the cowherd can enjoy with his/her age group to work in the field. The peer group will work in the jhum field, hitting the tilled-soil into soft-soil. When

Sekrenyi falls, they feast together and thereafter go to their respective duties again.

The parent will stop the cowherd from this profession after he/she has completed the minimum five years course of cattle keeping and begin to work in the field. According to the wisdom of the tradition, if one has prolonged the service of a cowherd, he/she will be late to learn the science of cultivation. Cultivation does not merely denote the rendering of physical labour for production of economic goods, it also includes learning the science of the soil, the proper selection of various seeds for a suitable soil, variable climatic condition of an area, the method of nurturing various crops, the periodic test of the soil for fresh cultivation etc. Furthermore, one has to learn the territorial boundary of the family land and other natural sources of income. The wisdom of the parent is that whatever he/she has learned out of the long time experience and the teachings of the parents, have to be taught to his/her children so that the same work culture, tradition and knowledge can be transmitted to future generations in continuity. Learning the science of cultivation and other life activities starts at about 16 years of age and end at about 24-25 years of age. This life training period that lasts for about 8-9 years is a significant course for career building. During this period the whole personality of a young man or woman is established. By the end of this period, they are eligible for marriage. Thereafter, a couple has to take the role of an independent family for future responsibilities of life.

As work culture is a continuous activity that governs every family in term of moral or duty bound life, there is no room for any sort of laziness, begging, starvation etc. No one stays at home during working days, except kids, very old men and woman, and sick people. Anyone, who is a delinquent, is treated 'shameful' and is segregated from association.

Division of Labour

Division of labour is apparent in Tenyimia society. The household activities, except any work that is to be done with tools-cum-armors such as dao, axe and spears are considered the duty of womenfolk. Work like construction of a house is considered heavy and as such classified as duty of men. Cooking, pounding of paddy, drawing water, washing, cleaning etc. at home are classified as the duty of the women. The mother is the treasurer of the family. She performs all family rituals at all occasions. Men-folks are responsible for village security, social harmony and anything related to social issues and judicial cases. Women are very industrious. They are responsible for the production of clothes of all the family members. The works in the field are allotted to all member of the family. Other small works such as black smithy, pottery, making basket and wooden-containers, making furniture and agricultural tools etc. are classified as the tasks of men folk. They are responsible for the sufficiency of such household goods of the family. Weaving is considered a primary profession of the women.

Other Occupations

There are certain other occupations in addition to agriculture. Production of sufficient foodstuff for the year is a pre-condition to all families in the community. Other occupational works are considered secondary. Those additional occupations are black smithy, carpentry, handicraft, pottery, yeast production, trading etc. although black smithy is a dependable trade for production of armors such as spear, sword, dao, etc. and other tools and implements for agriculture. Carpentry and other engineering works, are not regularly practiced or chosen. A village may have only one unit of black smithy and yet, except during dry season a smith will attend such minor works early in the morning and go to the field during the day. Making of household furniture is a male classified business and every male child has to learn it. Men folks are also responsible for making household necessities like various types of baskets – collecting baskets, carrying-baskets, storing-baskets, winnowing-plate, and plates, cups, spoons, etc. Pottery and yeast making are very rare. The common use of utensils during early life were earthen pots, earthen jars, earthen containers etc. Some people undertook trading as a secondary profession for the mercantile items such as jewels and armors. Khonoma villagers were famous because of their wide travels on such trading.

Engineering Works

Construction of family house, terrace fields and irrigations are the important engineering works of the ancestors. In all such works, neighbours and friends come to help the owner. The community streets are done in the form of social work. Each and every member of the village has the moral responsibility to extend voluntary help to other fellow members. As such, work culture has both personal and social ties in all walks of life.

Changes of Work Culture

As briefly mentioned earlier, the changes of traditional work culture is inevitable. The factors are manifold. The first and foremost factor is the spread of education and its seeking. Although, the spread of education is not even one and a half century old in Nagaland, education has led the Nagas, change their way of life, way of thinking and working system. The government servants with their monthly salary can afford to buy many things that attract the Nagas ranging from personal belongings, household assets and luxury items. The perks enjoyed by a government officer and their ability to serve society has a direct impact upon the mentality of the general masses. The spread of various governmental activities has motivated the people. The parents, despite facing numerous financial difficulties, wish their children to go for education so that they can become a responsible government officer. With such desire in mind, the parents, rich and poor send their children to schools for education, sacrificing the traditional work culture. This attitude of the general public becomes stronger and stronger as various level of white colour jobs multiply in government offices. The mentality of the educated class too do not promote traditional work culture. Their interest lies only in white collar jobs. The student life is difficult as one has to depend totally on the teaching of the teachers, as most parents are illiterate. There is no time to practice those practical works. The formative stage of every child requires theoretical knowledge. Moreover, their secondary age has to be spent in higher studies from another and far away locality, mainly in metropolitan cities, where there is no chance of thinking or learning traditional work rather then practicing it. Such mentality-gap and transient stage of life is gapped further by the increase of church activities in Naga society. It has been experienced that many people have the attitude of strong moral and spiritual obligation towards the church. As such, duties of personal, family of secular society, or even government duties are sacrificed for the church and related works. Many students also sacrifice their studies for spiritual service.

The modern form of trade and commerce is also a powerful factor in diminishing the traditional work culture. The modern industrial goods flow freely in society and are cheaper and attractive. The attention of the people, therefore has shifted to machine-made goods rather then self-producing pieces which are time consuming products.

Conclusion

Apart from all these psychological, internal and external factors, there are other factors such as political, professional etc. and the desire for higher economic status affect work culture. The political influence has led many people to acquire easy money and their hidden attitude has surpassed the value of dignity of labour. Many educated unemployed youth are never facilitated with proper implementation of national schemes such as NABARD, REDP etc. for rural unemployed youth. Government has no practical policy for promotion of trade and commerce. As such, even the few traditional craftsmen's products cannot find their way to the national markets. The revival of traditional work culture is a must to keep social and political harmony and to diminish anti-social elements. To achieve this, planning in various fields such as educational, social and economic is needed to transform the present Naga society. There is need to re-affirm and revitalize those ancestral 'work culture'.

REFERENCES

1. NEPED and IIPR, 1999, *Building of Traditional Agriculture in Nagaland,* India.
2. Virielhou and D.Koulie, 2001, *Tenyimia Tradition of Work Culture and Economy.*
3. Kekuodenuo and D.Koulie, 2001, *A Study of Traditional Law of Inheritance Tenyimia Society.*
4. Neizovinuo and Petekhrienuo, 2001, *The Role of Women in Tenyimia Society.*

9

Forces and Factors of Change in Naga Society[1]

Kekhrie Yhome

The Nagas are a very primitive and simple people and they have not forgotten their old ways of doing summary justice when they have a grievance against anyone. If you allow them to rule us or run the administration it will be a negation of justice or administration and it will be something like anarchy....
....They have not been able to chop off our heads for the last three thousand years and till 1948 they have not been able to do anything, and we are not afraid that they will chop off our head if they are not given independence of administration. It is a threat which is useless and worthless. We should not be frightened by these threats of some people who say that they will come down on us. This is intended to be imposed on us by the threats of some people, and we should be aware of these interested persons. There is no need to keep any Tribalstan away from us so that on times of trouble they will be helpful to our enemies.

Constituent Assemble Proceedings, Volume IX,
Monday, 8 August, 1949[2]

It has become a conventional methodology to identify the addition of new elements or the modification of existing "order"[3] by some "other"[4] elements as empirical departure to evaluate change, whether it is an "epistemological break" or "social change," and, again, it is this precise poverty of doing comprehensive justice to such an understanding that the crisis relating to the idea of "order" or "new" or "change" is always contested and marginalised into the debris of pedagogic enterprise as premises of foundational knowledge and, most paradoxically, value systems.

Therein, at the very outset, I would like to make it pertinent that a theme as histrionic as "Forces and Factors of Change in Naga Society" pose innumerable ambiguities as well as research inadequacies, and this is partially because the theoretical frame of investigations are not only epistemological but also imbibed with the onto-theological modes of European humanism. Similarly the conceptual and empirical bases of arguments on the agencies of affecting the "changes" are narrowly premised on the dominant nature of character of the disciplinary, multi-disciplinary, or interdisciplinary area under which the study attempts to locate itself. Thereof, any position paper assimilating these factors and forces as mathematical tools of investigation, whether it is the political, social, economic or otherwise, has been handicapped by the genealogical interpretation of modernity, and it is particularly this excess that the rationality of changes has always been overlooked by a possessive declaration of order and subservience as points of reference for interrogating any "changes," without calculating the very ontological or post-ontological premeditation of "change," with its ethical perspectives.

Having mentioned the apprehensions that are manifest in the "human sciences" or social sciences, another perspective that needs incorporation is the determination of "changes" itself, in relation to the individual and the "collective"[5]. For, the moment the theme announces "Naga," there is already the abrogated self-indignation that a suffering truth exists. This idea of "exists," or existence, however, should be carefully noted, partly because the anxieties of a Naga essence can be grossly miscalculated and also because the temptation to become a victim-hood of existential or cognitive sciences is very much felt. Rather, having disposed off the inadequacy or oversimplification of metaphysics, it is still a coveted argument to say that Nagas is a categorical marker of difference, by delimiting its relation to other differences, or by refusing to acknowledge the impossibility that announces Naga itself.

There are two cases that emerged from this problem:

1. The superimposed mythification or, rather, reification of the etymological interpretation that defines "Nagas" into a "society" or a "community."[6]
2. The cultural or historical materialism that creates a linear history of change and progress pattern of uninterrupted or inevitable processes, both of reaffirming existence with new modes of production, or changing/revolutionizing the older mode of production.

Firstly, the conceptualizing mechanism of the collective and the representative "Naga" is woven and made answerable to a representation or a signification of people by solely synchronizing or consolidating the etymological substantiation of the word itself.[7] The dynamics of identity formation or the evolution of identity, whether it is based on the principle of exclusiveness or uniqueness and the philosophical enterprise of difference, of the Nagas has been therefore interpreted through the etymological diffusion of the form and substance of a name, a concept, a word.[8] The casualty of creating an identity through naming has therefore remained central to any attempted distinction or reiterated assertion. It is also the signification or meaning that was extricated from a process of naming that the possibility of containing a collective, from another, was manufactured. In his interrogation of defining the process of consciousness for a community, Anderson remarks this modern disjunction as a process of the conflict between cosmology and history, which remains as one in the understanding of temporality in the pre-modern period.[9] over a period of time, or, rather, the lapses of periodical contamination with each other, there is an autolectic mechanism governed by the principle of European conception of time, whereby, all unnamed or unknown identities, when exposed to the metallurgical effects of rust or politics of number, begins to have immediate urgency, to have a consciousness, a name, defensive community.

Although Anderson articulated this frame of collective identity formation in the investigation of nationalism as a movement and a consciousness, what is central to his argument is the formation of a defensive mechanism in a collective "imagining," which is formed in the form of a collective consciousness through the formation of a homogeneous time (or "empty time"), when a "wedge is driven between cosmology and history."[10] Furthermore, what he has highlighted is also the nature of "time" in framing an auto-defensive identity based on a consciousness of change and naming process, the identification of a terrain that accepts or falls within the parameter of a certain commonality.[11] This is possible only through identification; and identification takes place in the sub-stratum regime or domain of signs. Louis Althusser, who also attempts to discredit "commodity fetishism" in the analysis of culture and society in Marxism, has defined this process in terms of "interpellation of the subject," where the unknown subject begins to assume significance the moment it is "hailed" by another authority or a superimposing institution. The sign or the name "Naga" therefore announces the vulnerability of an identity in relation to the other identity or (-ties). This relation is therefore a comparative approach because it is mathematical structure and fundamental by evaluation. This introduces and links us to the second case.

The second issue that has been challenging the changing patterns of a collective called Nagas is both measured in terms of its evolutionary process, (whether it is the Durkheimian or Turnerian approach), which was therein hastily imposed by statistical data and analytical intersections. This is loosely characterised and predominated by an arithmetic rationality or Hegelian judgement wherein teleological resultants of the "forces and factors" affecting changes are calculated by diminutively positioning the exterior values of a certain "modernity," or a certain juridical necessity of truth. It nevertheless remains to say that Engels indeed subscribed much to Hegel's judgement rather than Kant's speculation, and the relevance of this has also been incorporated into the dialectical interpretation of a linear Naga chronology, which is marked by re-interpretation of a progressive historical materialism.

The dialectics of Naga society was therein grounded in its very conceptual engineering of the "etymological scholarship" and this was not much of a crisis because the ordering of community was decided by transferring a process against a peculiar synchronisation. Similarly, the contradictions that were likely to emerge from such a status of indigenizing was also limited by the value orientation that were already operating – unlike the crisis that emerged in the European tradition, however outcome of this experience is the individual and the collective. An obvious conflict that has however come out of this experience is the attempted hybridisation of the etymological signification of the idea "Naga" and a shabbily reified enterprise premised on cultural materialism. The orthodoxy propounded in the materialisation of the word Naga,[12] particularly the ones linking the Nagas with other differential identities, on the one hand and, on the other, expands an alternative based on "immanence," which roots back to Heglian explication on problems of social theory. The continuity that was thereof appropriated through a definitional criteria or morphological assimilation of culturico-semantic lingualism introduced a discourse that posed to counter the hegemonic interpretation of a community as evolving and also as resisting the very perpetuation of such discourses.

Foremost to this aspect concerning a measured propensity, a mechanical ordering of preconceived assertions, is the aesthetics of the other in defining or in trying to compare. There existed a mutual interest in the mutual biological or cultural and material development of the Nagas affairs, whether it is the studies on changes of behavioural or cognitive culture, external developmental agencies like growth in literacy or patterns of work occupation, or ontologically defined areas like political consciousness and its subsequent turbulence. This pre-judicial assessment of the Nagas was limited by the need for policy-frames and the publishing industries or researches that facilitated any comprehensive studies are often based on the "self" and the "other" paradigms of pre-determination and pre-conception. Added to this is the geo-administrative status conferred to the Nagas was premised on the stern belief that the burden of the Self for the Other was a consistent feature and this legitimised the existing methodologies of research or structures of discourse. The ready-made factories of British or Indian colonial scholars re-searching on the Nagas was therefore one of the greatest casualties that shaped and formulated a systematic inquiry on the changes affecting the Nagas, and the factors and forces instigating such studies have been bounded by an inadequacy of information or a prejudicial motivation, to identify, legitimize and re-construct the Naga society.[13]

The conceptual as well as empirical outcomes dealing with this pattern of study on "changes" relies on three frameworks:

(i) The externalisation of the agency affecting change,

(ii) The internalisation of the agency affecting changes, and

(iii) The autopoeticisation of the agency.

Even in the methodological approaches highlighted above, the elements of "objective" and "subjective" explanations were not random but juxtaposed with more inclination towards the latter. This is because the Nagas never have any period called "modernity" in their history except that it was realised and propagated by others, basing on the subjective gaze. Charles Taylor[14] examines the difficulties by distinguishing two competing discourses – cultural and acultural – that has remained shrouded in the study of change as a peculiarity of modernity. The acultural theory describes "transformations" in terms of unspecified "culture-neutral operations," which sees examples like intellectual transformation "as a result of increased mobility, concentration of populations, industrialisation, etc., which are common to "every culture."[15] this approach also pre-supposes the deployment of "reason" as the chief faculty in determining changes as well as "transitions". This theory however remains ineffective because it "misclassify changes" and fails to "examine certain facets of the modern constellation, closely interwoven with our understandings of science and technology, that don't strike us as being part of the transformation to modernity"[16]. The second theory, which Taylor also supports, is the "cultural," which "supposes the point of view in which we see our own culture as one among others"[17].

Taylor's articulation on "change" fundamentally addressed an assertion for an ethical value whereby he says, "we need to draw from elsewhere our values and acceptable grounds for association with other." This grounding of opening is however a disoriented view because in the first place it strives to advocate and impose a certain conception of "democracy"[18] or social responsibility that is never inclusive and the very definition given to "modernity"[19] defines the very difference or infinite impossibility of any discourse on any objective situation. The violence of metaphysics, as Derrida[20] claims, was inherently woven into the fabric of every discourse, which revolves between valorisation or aestheticisation and as occasional papers, and it is the perpetuation of discourse that conveys the parochial definition or exemplary introduction to modernity, as the case study of "forces and factors" implicates.

The "collective" struggle for power to self-determine, like the discourse in postcolonial studies, constitute the core of any epistemological interrogations, which, much before, has had been already supplemented by the defining consciousness of colonial domination. The communitisation of an "empty signifier" as a perpetuating discourse of signification and a dialectical process was therefore one among the most primary important change in the history of ideas concerning the entity called Nagas[21]. For clarification purpose the reference used in this paper as "Naga society" is therefore an indication that a substantiated "signified" is already grounded, by and large in the imagination as well as in the socio-economic, politico-historical, or geo-strategic spheres of relationship and correlationship. The announcement of "Naga society" therefore announces the temperament of a linear progressive identity or community that is subjected by conditions of historical materialism; a "cohesive society" responding to "global phenomena"[22]. The appropriation of "society", which Bourdieu calls as "habitus,"[23] is also seen in European phenomenon whereby the need to conceptually distinguish in the "social sciences" the relationship between State and the People became apparent in the form of State and Society[24].

For again, the other division that remains critical in the analysis of "society" is the emergent assumption on "civil society." The post-Hobbesian till the market autonomy collated in Europe generated an opinion on resurgent civil society and it also saw the consolidation of its discourse shaped by its protestant ethic, which was challenged among many others.[25] This particular momentum was also marked by a gradual response in the form of analyzing colonial practices and its impact,[26] or the sharp denial of contradicting civil society and elitist opinions.[27] The framing of the periods, epochs, causation, assimilation, and it appeared quite rudimentary, and it assumed to have outlined a Naga discourse. The identification and stabilisation of a subject-identity through the discourse of society and community has come to have important ramifications on the epistemological variability of determining changes.[28]

The practices of "foundational epistemology" dates from Locke to Descartes and the prevailing enthocentracism are visible on the basis of an identity that was established in relation to other existing identities. The case of the Nagas is also a matter of this challenge because there are other proper names like the Kukis or Meiteis or the Assamese, for particular mentioning, although the basis of identity formation was partly because of institutionalised (or State) mechanisms. An author has argued that the spatio-temporal set-up of the Indian State, its "environmental milieu," and the relational contradictions which re-organises into "empirical possibilities" on the basis of such existing (or institutional) power means and ends as equitable with the legitimacy or contrary, what is interesting is the idea of "democracy" and "traditional" as two competing assertions in the search for individual and collective resistance/ response against the tyranny of State ideology.[30]

In locating the fringe of violence in a discourse that shaped the collective imagination of the Nagas, there are certain questionings relating to the "subaltern" collective, the movement of the collective, and the desiring antagonism that bridges the collective and the movement, and the topological forces that created a mechanism for the very violence of language. There are anthropological offshoots attempting to integrate the cognitive social with the geostrategic, as in Burman Roy, who argues that "schizophrenic alienation" (including the Nagas) is rooted in "geography, in history, in somatic traits"[31]. Another author has imposed the need of a drastic break (revolution would have been a better word) in an institutionalised situation – "by successfully terminating the life of the colonial state, nationalism could be carried forward only by superseding the conditions of colonial rule"[32]. However, even the post-modern thinkers have often felt this perplexing and often contradicting positions. Appadurai says that for "deterritorialised groups to think their way out of the imaginary of the nation-states is itself the cause of much global violence since many movements of emancipation and identity are forced, in their struggles against existing nation-states, to embrace the vary imaginary they seek to escape"[33]. The question of Naga identity is constrained by this very impetus[34].

An analysis of any "collective" is therefore marked by the apparent Hegelian synthesis to compare, be it the paradigmatic or syntagmetic mode, which nonetheless often results in an inability to contemplate on the exigency defining change. In highlighting the intellectual developments and the consequentiality of "time," as imperative exigencies in the given preview of "forces and factors of changes in Naga Society," there is a need to integrate the fundamentals of ethical values, the role of the imaginary (whether it is a relationship between the past and present – as tradition and change implies; or between the present and the future – as the construction of "continuity" in social change implicates; or, finally, between the past and the future, as the incorporation of values and *mythos* establish).

It was Walter Benjamin[35] who introduced the thought of locating the concept of progress from the vestiges of history, which is at once a mythical realm and distorted version, and this remarkably, differs from what Max Weber denounces as a preoccupation of disenchantment. Most of Benjamin's work discerns with urban spaces but the element of public spheres make it pertinent to mention how objects and images of the past can be re-framed, or what it concerns. The main lacunae that Benjamin targets is the social democratic belief that history is progressing, which also attempts to bring a reified consciousness among the "working class the role of the redeemer of future generations, in this way cutting the sinews of its greatest strength. For this training made the working class forget both its hatred and its spirit of sacrifice, both are nourished by the images of enslaved ancestors rather than that of liberated grand children"[36]. The conditions relating to an inevitable crisscrossing with the past, which is already there in the mind, as Wittgenstein mentions about it, has also become the turning frame of ethical perspectives in trying to correlate the past changes as from now.

For the controversial thinker Martin Heidegger, history is not a matter of the past as inasmuch it is for the present but, rather, history is grounded in the future[37]. In response and defiance against Heidegger, Deeleuze argues that repetition is not a continuity but a discontinuity with the past[38]. In the study of history, we are therefore confronted with the issues of remembering and the politics of selective remembering or amnesia. Similarly, in the course of historical materialism, the changes that affects or is chronologised with a systematic chain of cohesiveness and coherence, which we have already demarcated, is rooted in "foundational epistemology." The agencies that are interpreted in this epistemological grounding have also been argued, which Taylor also asserts: "changes are partly understood in terms of the loss of traditional beliefs, either because they are undermined by the growth of reason or because they are marginalised by institutional change"[39]. The tantamount point of departure thereon shaping an ethical perspective towards the evaluation of the "past" is through the approaches that exemplify an immanent critique. This also introduces us to the western tradition conception of time.

There are two traditions in the interpretation of time: the classical/Hellenic representation, which is marked as circular, and the Christian concept of time, which has challenged the classical notion, is of a straight line. For the first time is conceived as eternal whereas the second values the eternal return, the predominant Christian belief. Therefore the onto-theological enterprise that swayed the European mode of metaphysics and thinking is based in the belief that the world, as Peuch remarks, "is created within time and must end within time." The yearning for a return, a past, the unliveable and non quantifiable experiences, has two major trusts: the immanence of nostalgia in the very thinking systems, which was introduced in modern times through German Romanticism, and the explication of the past experience as a mode of reproducing "memory." This nostalgia for the past can be accounted as a loss felt by the subject exemplifying the tragedy of modern space, seeking for an answer in the past for the continuity of the present, which Kant too felt the need for and was re-affirmed by Schiller.[40] The site of "pure immanence" in the western metaphysics was therein resurrected in the conformity of adhering to the limits of the ontotheological conception of time.

In his analysis of social reproduction, Marx also could not go beyond this tradition, feels Agamben, "every conception of history is invariably accompanied by a certain experience of time which is implicit in it, conditions it, and thereby has to be elucidated. Similarly, every culture is first and foremost a particular experience of time, and no new culture is possible without an alteration in this experience. The original task of a genuine revolution, therefore, is never merely to 'change the world' [as in Marx], but also – and above all – to 'change time'"[41]. The European model of arresting historical materialism has been displaced by the invariable diffusion of "time" and the ethical predicament of change has come to challenge us more than any time because the understanding of different plural societies have already been entertained through the philosophical evaluation of community. It remains inasmuch a matter of how we construct, reconstruct and endure the Naga experience: whether it remains struck by the predators of European thought, or whether Nagas are "becoming", to use Heidegger's term, or in the process of affirming the space it has been constrained with.

REFERENCES

1. This paper, based on given theme, was presented during a seminar "Continuity and Change in Naga Society," at the Department of History and Archaeology, Nagaland University, Kohima, in collaboration with MAKAIAS, Kolkota, from 3-4 December, 2002.
2. http://alfa.nic.in/debates.vol9p7b.htm
3. Michael Focult has used the analysis of knowledge and power in the background of a particular institutional "order", over the period of change, most vociferously. See Michael Focult, *The Order of*

Things: An Archaeology of the Human Science,(tr.) Alan Sheridan(New York: Pantheon Books,1970).

4. The notion of the "other" has been used extensively in post-colonial studies as well as other social sciences. The deriving energy for this notion is based inasmuch on the Freudian definitions whereby the Ego matures or moves into public spheres of recognition of the Self, passing through the "mirror stage". I have however used the Other as a categorical marker, which presupposes the cosmological and real time; the ones which finds concepts in nostalgia, reflection, transition, change, progress, praxis, etc., all attached with the peculiarity of a certain spatio-temporal order.
5. I have used "collective" inter-changeably with "society" although "community" is the most preferred concept to define the cumbersome politics of number and consensual democracy.
6. The semiotic process of naming in a "colonial situation," says Southall, assumes greater significance because "name was fundamental. For if you had no name you did not exist, so if you could not produce a name, one would be found and forced upon you, with a name that the colonial power recognised, even if you did not, you begin to claim rights, collective personality and territory.' See Aidan Southall, "Tribe," in David Levinson and Melven Ember (eds) *Encyclopaedia of Cultural Anthropology,* Vol. 4 (New York: 1996), pp. 1332-33.
7. This problem is the relation from word to idea to thing had been first introduced by the eleven century philosopher Pierre Abelard.
8. "Existing anthro*mimetic* references and narrative industries attempt to arrive at a conclusion for defining the word "Naga". Verrier Elwin defines 'Naga' as a phonetic retardation of 'Nok' or people, as in western Burma languages; Hutton's 'Noga' was mentioned to be a corruption of Assamese's naked'; Lt. Col. Waddel Sanskritised it as 'Nag', meaning a mountain and therefore mountain-people primates; Mr. Peal's eastern Naga interpretation of 'Nok' as a people; or, finally, Hokishe Sema's 'Na-Ka' as a word communicating perforation of earlobes, is a more subtler but cultural material hermeneutism. The 'Buranjis' or Ahom Kingdom chronicles anyhow described it as 'Noga', not from its etymological or cultural materialism point of view, but from an anthro-geo-ontological intersectioning of culturico-commodified tagging." See Kekhrie Yhome, "The Irreducible Object-Crisis of Being Identified Naga and the Anthro-Military Subject of the Name," Unpublished

Monograph, 2002 fall.

9. See Benedict Anderson, *Imagined Communities: Reflections on the Origin and Spread of Nationalism* (London: Verso, 1983)
10. *Ibid.*, p. 36.
11. An explanation to this has been already provided by Hannah Arendt by studying the relation of violence and "polemology" or "instincts of 'group territorialism," in *On Violence* (London: Allen Lane The Penguin Press, 1969).
12. Hokishe Sema first introduces this particular shift from the etymological approach, in his explanation on the expression "Naka", in *Emergence of Nagaland :Socio-Economic and Political Transformation and the Future* (New Delhi: Vikas Publishing House Pvt. Ltd., 1986), p. 3.
13. Verrier Elwin, among all others, is quoted here because he influenced and shaped Nehru in many ways, particularly after the latter's open anger and "hatred" against the Naga: "Elwin privately described in his book Nagaland as attempting 'in a subtle and dispassionate way as possible to put, India' case on all matters above which there has been controversy'- matters such as treating of minority in India as a whole, the legitimacy of India's claim over the Naga territory, the representatives, or the lack of it, of the Naga insurgents, and the truth of the allegation regarding{Indian} army brutality." Elwin, then, went ahead on distorting the Naga, which were recounted in that "All his life elwin had to work his way between competing allegiance……yet the Nagaland assignment presented a dilemma of almost unsurpassed painfulness."

    See Ramachandra Guha, *Savaging the Civilised: Verrier Elwin, His Tribals, and India* (New Delhi: Oxford University Press, 2000), pp. 285-87.
14. Charles Taylor, "Two Theories of Modernity," in *Public Culture*, Vol.11, No.1, 1999, pp. 153-74.
15. *Ibid.*, p. 154.
16. *Ibid.*, p. 160
17. *Ibid.*, p. 158.
18. The concept of Democracy is not a fixed meaning or its ethical paradigms binding. It has a deeper underlying meaning because it is a provisional description, for a certain advantage.
19. "Modernity," outlines Taylor, "is charaterised by the loss of the horizon; by a loss of roots; by the hubris that denies human limits,

our dependence on history or God, that places unlimited confidence in the powers of frail human reason; by trivializing self-indulgence that has no stomach for the heroic dimensions of life; and so on."

20. Jacques Derrida, "Violence and Metaphysics," in *Writing and Difference, (tr)* Alan Bass (Chicago: Chicago University Press, 1978)
21. An author has polemically posited this calculation in a categorical statement: "...fifty years of suppressive actions and atrocities perpetuated by the instruments of the Indian state had created a profile of an 'oppressed nation' seeking their rightful place in the international community of liberated nations in ongoing processes of decolonisation." See Lokendra Arambam, *MRFD Bulletin*, Vol.1, Issue 4, Manipur Research forum, Delhi, December 2001, p. 11.
22. Ahu Sakhrie, "Naga Nationalism: Differences and Perspectives," in *Kohima College Silver Jubilee Souvenir*, Kohima College, 1967-1992, pp. 27-34.
23. A "habitus" or embodied understanding is seen as a social understanding (as separate from the natural ordering) of existence and relationship since the systems of society create an understanding and reflection of its own. See Pierre Bourdieu, *Outline of a Theory of Practice* (Cambridge: Cambridge University Press, 1977)
24. Dennish H.Wrong, "Reflections on the death of Socialism: changing perceptions of the state/society line," in *Theory and Culture*, Vol. 29, 2000, pp. 175-85.
25. Following Jean-Paul Sartre's incision on "extentialism," the predominant intellectuals that emerged in answer to Western appropriation of its discourse includes Frantz Fanon, *Wretched of the Earth*(tr.) C. Farrington (New York: Grove Press, 1963) and Edward W. said, *Orientalism: Western Conception of the Orient* (London; Henley: Routledge and Kegan Paul, 1978) and, latter, the "subaltern" school of thought.
26. See Piketo Sema, *British Policy and Administration in Nagaland, 1881-1947* (New Delhi: Scholar Publishing House, 1991).
27. The theme for the 125 years of Christianity in Naga areas celebration was "From Darkness to Light." This highly sonotous and value laden caricature depicts a Bachelardian "paradigm shift" – a colossal branding of fore-parents as "savages," "headhunters," "barbarians," etc. – to a more etiquette mis-identification of Pareto's

"circulation of elite." Also, see, Nagaland Pradesh Congress Committee, *Bedrock of Naga Society*, Kohima, 2000; Nagaland Baptist Church Council, *Nagaland Celebrates Quasqui Centennial*, Kohima, 1997.

28. *Op cit.*, Kekhrie Yhome, Unpublished Monograph.
30. *Ibid*, p. 139
31. Burman Roy, B.K. , "For Overcoming the Schizophernic Alienation of the North-East: Outline of a Comprehensive Approach," *Mainstream*, October 27, 2002, pp. 13-19.
32. Partha Chatterjee, *The Nation and its Fragments: Colonial and Postcolonial Histories* (New Delhi: Oxford University Press, 1993),p. 26.
33. Arjun Appadurai, "Patriotism and Its Future," in *Public Culture*, Vol. 5, No. 3, 1993, p. 418.
34. The autopoetic character, or the ability to self-reproduce, without any internal or external agency, can be contested here.
35. Walter Benjamin, *The Arcades Project*, (tr.) Howard Eiland and Kevin MacLaughlin (Cambridge: The Belknap Press of Harvard University Press, 1999).
36. Wlater Benjamin, "Theses on the Philosophy of History," in *Illuminations*, (ed.) Hannah Arendt (New York:Shocken Books, 1968), p. 260.
37. "The happening and the happenings of history are primordially and always the future, that in a concealed way comes towards us, a revelatory process that puts us at risk, and thus is compelling in advance. The future is the beginning of all happening. Everything is enclosed within the beginning." See Martin Heidegger, *Basic Questions of Philosophy* (Bloomington; Indianapolis: Indiana University Press, 1992), p. 35.
38. Gilles Deleuze, *Difference and Repetition*, (tr.) Paul Patton (London:The Athlone Press, 1994), pp. 200-201.
39. See Charles Taylor, *op cit.*, p. 169.
40. Jacques Tamminaux, *Poetics, Speculation, and Judgement: the Shadow of the Work of Art from Kant to Phenomenology*, (tr.) Michael Gendre (Albany: State University of New York, 1993)
41. Girogio Agamben, *Infancy and History: The Destruction of Experience*, (tr.) Liz Heron (London; New York:Verso, 1993), p. 91.

10

Administrative and Social Factors

The Change in Naga Society

Charles Chasie

Introduction

It is difficult subject because the Nagas are a conglomeration of different tribes with different cultures, traditions, languages, value systems etc. and the forces of change as well as the degree of affectation have not only been varying for different tribes but they have also happened at different times. It is also these very diversities and the fact that a workshop like today's is a seminal attempt to properly delve into our past, in order to understand better our present, which make it interesting also. And, it is through attempts like this that we will begin to map out our course, as a people, to the future.

The seminar has used the phrase "Naga Society" but author would like to approach the subject from ground level zero and from the premise that Nagas, most probably, were not one people until the recent past. This does not mean that Nagas should not become one people. We should. The purpose in approaching the subject from such a stand-point is to provide a clearer perspective. And one is having to do this because there is some disinclination among our people to go deeper into this issue while the tendency is to talk about an unclear common past and even to glorify it. Such tendencies are harmful and dangerous because they prevent better understanding about the past and block our progress into the future. And they create a mind-set that is no longer open and objective.

What are the facts about Nagas we have?

i) There are many different tribes who are either recognised as Nagas or they call themselves 'Naga'. However, till date, there is no authoritative version of the number of Naga tribes.

ii) There was no such thing as 'Naga Society', may be not even Tribe Society. We had Village Societies, even Republics, each warring with the other although, sometimes, also conducting their affairs on a very high order.

iii) The term "Naga" itself is still shrouded in mystery and open to various interpretations.

iv) The origins of the Naga tribes are still unknown. Many tribes can trace the route of their migration back to Makhel and Khezhakenoma villages. But beyond this, there is complete blank. And while most Naga tribes believe their ancestors came from below ground, there is at least one tribe that believes their ancestors came from Water.

v) The process of the tribes forming themselves into people, following the advent of the British, may be said to be continuing. In 1929, nearly a century after the British first set foot on Naga soil, the Kukis were accepted as Nagas by the other tribes[1]. But, today, they are no longer recognised as Nagas. Even now, we read disturbing newspaper reports of claims and disclaimers about certain tribes being Nagas.

So, this is the kind of scenario under which we are discussing the forces and factors of change in Naga Society.

Various Forces and Factors of Change

The first known major change affecting the Naga tribes was the Treaty of Yandabo, in 1826, even before the British set foot on Naga soil in 1832[2]. This Treaty divided the Naga areas into Burma and British India and started the process of fragmentation and Balkanisation of the tribes that were soon to become known as the Naga people. Their actual arrival, in some ways, deepened the division because their presence not only created conflict of loyalties among the tribesmen who remained under their administration but also some areas, even on the British Indian side of the border remained beyond the reach of British Administration and were called "Un-administered Areas"[3]. In some other ways, it helped the Nagas to come together because there were cases of several villages banding together to fight the British[4]. Not surprisingly, their presence also exposed the Naga hillsmen to a different way of life.

The biggest contributions of British administration at the time were the introduction of a system of justice that could be applied uniformly to all Naga tribes, the use of "money" and travel with a measure of security. Many Naga tribesmen started to travel to different parts of British India, such as Dacca, Ceylon, Cambay, Karachi etc., trading in ornamental jewellery and other goods. The other contribution was the recruitment of Nagas into the Allied Labour Corps during the World War I, and sending them to France[5], which may have helped plant the seed of Naga "peoplehood" as the realisation of the concept of nations dawned on them. On the whole, however, the British left the Nagas much to themselves and their way of life.

What actually affected the Nagas and their way of life more was what came in the footsteps of the British – the

Christian Missionaries, conversion and education, even a script to enable written communication, followed. The world of the Naga was now truly turned upside down as beliefs and value systems changed, traditional institutions and practices on which depended the fabric of society were undermined and relegated to the background, lifestyles changed, new habits formed etc. The inability of some early missionaries to appreciate Naga beliefs and values and to build on them made things worse. All Naga beliefs and cultural practices were looked upon as pagan and to be shunned. They introduced change but this change threatened to completely severe all vital links to our people's cultural and historical roots. Naturally, there was much resistance to the spread of the Christian message, initially, and some early Naga converts were even disowned and exiled from their village communities. The price the early Naga Christians had to pay for their beliefs was high. Unfortunately, today, in some village communities, instead of showing Christian forgiveness, grace, and respect for their own roots, there is a tendency among the majority Christian members to try to impose their wills on the entire community. Such tendencies are, sometimes, witnessed even on bigger scales. Some may strongly react to what I have said here but I have done so because I respect commitment to faith of the early Naga Christians and I have no wish to see the high cost they had to pay for their faith cheapened. And I am aware that the burden of history and the magnitude of the responsibility that the Church bears towards Naga society, especially in the context of where Naga society has reached today, must weigh heavily on those Church leaders who understand.

In the immediate aftermath of the World War I, and Naga exposure in France as Allied Labour, the formation of the Naga club took place back home in Kohima by the then Naga civil servants and educated[6] class. This Naga club was to take a historic step in 1929, setting the Nagas on a road of irreversible political journey, when they signed their famous memorandum to the Simon Commission, asking the British to either keep the Naga areas under their direct administration or, if this was not possible, to leave them as they were before the British arrived[7]. The Naga issue, sometimes called the Naga Political Problem, is a legacy of this Memorandum to the Simon Commission.

If World War I exposed a few thousand Nagas to the birth pangs of a new world order, the World War II brought it to Naga soil. After this experience of being a major theatre of the War, the Nagas could not remain the same ever again. The world was brought to their doorstep and, to that extent, the Naga world also shrank even while his view expanded. Unfortunately, this was not just a measured acceleration but a sudden quantum leap into the unknown. For instance, even before the Nagas could become familiar with the Money Economy, from the Barter System from which they were just beginning to emerge, War Economy had overtaken them. One result is that Nagas never learnt the true value of money and what it does or how to properly manage their resources. On the other hand, Naga society has continued to fight a losing battle against inflation, and inflationary trends ever since. The cycle is represented, today by —High cost and style of living – corruption – Deficits over revenue – Lack of investment – Inadequate production – Inflation etc.

The coming of Statehood, and it's existence over four decades, and the introduction of so-called planned economy and development, have been helpless in breaking this cycle in a situation where the people do not know any better. Hence, we have in Nagaland, what is better known as the Conveyor Belt Economy of cash transfers from Delhi to Kohima and back to Delhi! The rise in unemployment and the entrenched conflict situation have only made more difficult any attempts to salvage what has already been an intractable case scenario.

In such manner, ever since, Naga people have always had to contend with the succession of events which overtake them even before they can even digest and assimilate the previous ones. The consequence is lack of breathing space and inability to deal adequately with events. Indeed, Nagas have been barely able to react to events as they happen. The only things that have sustained them so far have been the fact that they have only so recently emerged from the solidity of their cultural homesteads, their own resilience and their ability to laugh and make light of their adversities. Tragically, the prolonged period of conflict, and fratricidal killings, are slowly but surely taking away their sense of humour and generating much bitterness. And unless the Churches, and Naga leaders, are wise, the Naga sense of identity could further suffer severe jolts.

Finally, all Nagas are trapped within the Naga political Issue. And there will be no escape from it for anyone until a workable settlement is found. There is no part of Naga life and society which has not been touched by this Issue and the tentacles from it. You will also notice that I preceded the word "settlement" with the word "workable". What do I mean by it? It means that all groups and all sections of Naga society must be properly, if only broadly, included. For this to happen, the past must be consciously revisited, wrongs and injustices done then must be acknowledged, restitution made and the wounds healed. A broad consensus can then emerge across the table and above-board. So long as this does not happen, clever stratagems may be made, situations and people may be manipulated to suit one's purposes, but no amount of Accords or Settlements, contrived through such short cut methods, will work in the long term. And the issue will keep re-surfacing from the ashes of the last Accord/ Settlement because Naga "Peoplehood"[8] and the Naga Political Issue, for good or ill, were built on the same foundation. The bitterness each such Accord generates will also be more entrenched than the one before.

Let us look at the scenario we have, today, before us. We have a conglomeration of tribes who claim, even stridently, to be a people but who have little concept of how they came to be a people. In the meantime, most of our people are unable to go beyond their personal and group/tribe interests and little sense of attachment or loyalty further than that. We also know little about the languages, cultures or values of the other tribes, and the interest level to really learn about the other tribes is very low. And there is hardly any positive inter-tribal exchange except from the bitter end of anger and ill feeling. We desperately need a blueprint, beyond political slogans, on how we can become a people. In a meeting of Nagas from all over the Naga areas, in Kohima in August, 2001, when there was a talk about Nagas being one, a Konyak leader asked "Are we? Can we?" Such questions have become desperately urgent and vital if we are to translate our claims into reality.

We created a Cause before we could fully become a people. This was alright if it helped us to become a people. And initially, the Cause did accelerate the process of our tribes coming together. But the Cause, for various reasons, soon preceded the process of our becoming a people and seemed to have gone on it's own. The building of our nationhood got neglected and even began to slide backwards. What further accentuated this neglect was the explanation that out nationhood was already a fact and that our people would automatically unite and become one, cooperating with each other, once the Cause was achieved. The logical extension of such thinking process is that only a few "traitors" were standing in the way. This, from the standpoint of our nationhood, is not only bereft of reality but also dangerous because it promotes the ideology that the end justifies the means and leads to physical elimination of those whom we perceive are standing in our way. We have all seen enough evidences of this without further elaboration. We forgot that a palace cannot be built without firm foundation at the base. The result is that, although many of us may still refuse to accept our nationhood and our becoming a people of now, lie under threat while the possibility of a mushrooming of warlords and inter-tribal enmity, and a ground situation not unlike those in Afghanistan or Rwanda and Burundi, stares us in the face.

Why have we reached such a stage where our people have become our own worst enemies? Where our people call the Government of India, even India as a country, our enemy but continue to kill Nagas? Because there has been few meeting points between our political aspirations and the mental and spiritual growth of our people which are needed to translate our aspirations into fact and reality. You simply can't build a nation without massive continuous nation-building works.

In such a situation what have become the biggest and most potent forces and factors of change? Personal ambition, interests of the self, of the group and tribe as well as fear, suspicion, bitterness and spite. And, above all, our reactions, largely prompted by these feelings. The Who has become more important than the What. Our negative urges seem to have taken precedence over our positive instincts. The result of all these is that we are fast becoming a sterile people, able only to talk about the past and past achievements with little ability to think ahead and go forward.

We need to put back nation building, and the process of our tribes becoming a people, at the top of our agenda. This is more important than political sloganeering, overground or underground. We need to go back to our roots and build on our cultural heritages. And we need to reach out to one another. But how do we do this after all that has happened and the wear and tear that have already taken place in our relationships? We must create the space for a level-playing field where no one feels threatened and where everyone, big or small, can converge on equal footing. And the only way to do this is to forgive and be forgiven, realizing that we are all human and bound to make mistakes. We need to consciously revisit the past and heal the wounds that we have inflicted on one another through seeking forgiveness, making restitution where possible, and being reconciled. If we do these, God and our people will come into the center of our scheme of things again. And they will clear the debris now cluttering our collective path and help us to, once more, walk forward as a people with assurance and dignity. Some people say that reconciliation can take place after a political settlement. I, personally, do not think so. Instead, the question arises," Can there be a workable political settlement without reconciliation and healing and carrying our people with us?" In some other parts of the world, political settlements have come as a result, directly or indirectly, of external pressure. But the geo-politics and the dynamics of our situation are different from those other conflict situations and our people cannot hope that the same results can be effected in like manner. In our situation, there is no alternative to reconciliation. We may talk about peace and unity but neither will be available without reconciliation.

Sense of History

The task assigned to me has been largely to interpret and assess our people's recent history in order to understand the present better with, perhaps, the hope that we might also gain some insights into the future. And I have given my understanding of what happened and where I think we are. But interpreting history has many limitations and depends on many factors mainly in relation to who is doing the interpretation. This is why almost always there are several versions of history. And, at the most, we have an official version, which we sanctify by calling it "authoritative". If interpreting and analyzing history is difficult, to do the same for the present is near impossible, and almost always prove pre-mature over time. But these efforts are a must because they help us to reflect and to distil the substance from the many details and the confusion over them.

What is, however, even more important than interpretations of history, in my mind, is to have a sense of history and destiny. Those who have a sense of history will also have clear perspectives. History is also usually made by them. I do not, of course, suggest that only they make history. For instance, in the case of a person like Hitler, who made world history in such a forceful manner, one could very well ask whether it was a sense of history or sheer personal ambition, which propelled him. He led Germany to ruin. More recently, Anwar Sadat's olive branch to Israel proved controversial in the Arab world, and even led to his own assassination. But Egypt regained its honour and the world's respect and approbation. Likewise, we can think of Piere Mendez of France and Robert Schumacher of France, Chancellor Konrad Adenaur of Germany, Prime Minister Kishi of Japan, India's own Mahatma Gandhi etc.

The Naga people are where they are today because of the sense of history of those Naga leaders who signed the memorandum to the Simon Commission. I also hold the belief that if our present crop of Naga leaders imbibe in themselves a sense of history and destiny for our people, undiluted by their own personal ambitions and manipulations, they could cause a paradigm shift in our situation and have the Naga Issue settled in a way that is both honourable and acceptable to our people. Such a workable settlement could also come sooner than present situation indicates. But unless this happens, I am afraid, our people's hopes and expectations would be raised every time only to be hopelessly dashed again. The Issue will also keep getting more entrenched and complicated to settle each time.

History and time do not belong to anyone. We cannot manipulate them however much we may try or think we can. They will still be there long after we are gone. What we can do is to learn from them so that we do not keep repeating past mistakes.

REFERENCES

1. Naga Club, 1929, *Memorandum to Simon Commission*, Text available in various publications including *The Naga Imbbroglio* by Charles Chasie.
2. Chasie, Charles, 1999, *The Naga Imbroglio : A Personal Perspective*, Standard Printers and Publishers, 1999.
3. Elwin, Verrier, 1969, *The Nagas in the Nineteenth Century*, Oxford University Press.
4. *Ibid.*
5. Yonuo, Asoso, 1974, *The Rising Nagas: A Historical, Political Study*, Vivek Publishing House, Delhi.
6. Chasie, Charles, 1999. *The Naga Imbroglio.*
7. See Text of Memorandum to Simon Commission.
8. Burman, Roy, Nagas and Peace Prospects, *Mainstream*, July 22, 2000.

11

World View and Transformation

Aküm Longchari

Creating Meaning:

> 'Of all our studies, history is well qualified
> to reward our research' —*Malcolm X*

One of the utmost and consistent historical forces that profoundly influences and guides the human journey and collective transformation of a peoples' continues to be their 'world-view'. Indeed the forces of history and world-view influence each other through a subtle interplay of human progression. It is our worldview that help us to create meaning to the world that we see around us and defines our responses to it. However, it would not be unfair to mention that the functions and decisiveness of world-view in sharing Continuity and Change has neither been adequately recognised nor made comprehensible.

This discussion is animated around the culture of Continuity and Change that is inspired by the forces of worldview which guides patterns of human interaction and human relationship with fellow humans, with nature and with the supernatural. With critical and honest reflection let us in this gathering hold true to Bantu Steve Biko who reminds us that *"As people existing in a continuous struggle for truth, we have to examine and question old values and systems."*

Let us not trivialize the significance of how a world view determines our response to the realities around us, because by doing so we tend to take for granted indigenous worldviews and cultures, knowledge systems and realities and therefore continue betraying the struggle for trans\formation of the poor and oppressed people's movement to attain basic needs, right to life and freedom.

Richard Hooker tells us that "world view" is a set of propositions and perspectives about the organisation and often the hierarchies of the material, immaterial, and social worlds. World view is a complex, dynamic, and often contradictory series of interrelated ideas, observations, symbols and practices that in their entirety define a culture and the individuals within that culture.

Anthropologist Michael Kearney provides a useful working meaning that states "world view" as a way of looking at reality consisting of basic assumptions and images that provide a more of less coherent, though not necessarily accurate, way of thinking about the world.

It is often a people's culture that lays the foundation of a people. World view is the cause and product of Continuity and Change which is found in narratives, the material world, the social world and the symbolic world. Therefore it is imperative to recognize that a people's worldview translates into how people organize themselves. It is their worldview that determines how they define and evolve systems, institutions, policies, education; models of governance and parameters of relation to other nations in their ever-continued search to be makers of their own culture.

Depending on how we understand and define 'culture' we

create and give meaning to the term 'world view'. In other words it is our culture that defines the nature and usage of 'world view' in the context of a peoples' perception of its realities and its response to Continuity and Change. Therefore to create a meaningful understanding of how world view shapes Continuity and Change, let me spend a few moments sharing with you how Babu Ayindo and Aküm Longchari in their paper "From Cold War to Hot Peace?" grapple with the simple yet often very confusing term "Culture"- which is at the core of human interaction.

A Perspective on Culture

> 'We are not fighting for integration...
> We are fighting for recognition as human beings'
> —*Malcolm X*

It seems that dependent upon one's intention and motive, the definition one gives to the word 'culture' can either push a people's capacity to become makers of history or, as is all too commonly experienced, send them to a museum as spectators of history. Many definitions of culture favour the reductionist perspective that sustains the *status quo* by selectively slicing away events and activities and, above all, commodifying them. With such narrow definitions of culture, it is not surprising that whenever young people from third world assert the power of their culture they are greeted by the cynical refrain: "You mean you want to go back to wear skins, sticking spears through each other and sleeping on trees?"

Again, the written history of third and fourth world people written as it was with questionable intentions – is full of violent interpretations and prejudices that strips away a peoples dignity and humanity. Little is said about the oral history that has narratives that recognizes the richness of a people's culture and affirms the life embracing values that our ancestors evolved by way of nation building and peacemaking. Instead, our ancestors are depicted as nothing more than a violent, blood thirsty "natives". And if there is any good at all then it is "tribal" and not effective in the "modern era".

Bantu Steve Biko defined culture as "the society's composite answer to the varied problems of life". And more importantly, "we are experiencing new problems everyday and whatever we do adds to the richness of our cultural heritage, as long as it has humans as its center."[1] Indeed, the etymology of the term denotes dynamism and a state of permanent continuous transformation. As Bennars and Njoroge inform us that "culture" comes from Latin word "cultus" which means to cultivate, or more precisely, act upon the land, transforming it for production. "Cultus" involves human action to transform the world, to make the world human.[2] This explains why for indigenous people land is central to their definition of culture and who they are – and who they are not – for as the 2020 activists put it, "each culture explains a particular relationship to the land."[3]

Broadly speaking, therefore, culture entails human response to three important elements: nature, fellow humans and the world beyond or the supernatural. Through reflection and action, a people – any people- would constantly be in the process of negotiating the evolving culture and challenges that emerge from the three elements. It is this capacity to be makers of culture that differentiates humans from animals. "To make culture," Augusto Boal notes, "is to invent the world so that it responds to our needs, our desires, and our dream."[4] And indeed it is the power of cultures that shape our world views in our response to creating change.

In today's so-called modern era of globalism and

universalism we have witnessed humanity evolve a culture that does enhance life. Culture has lost its dynamism and the power of culture is no longer being felt as a deciding factor in shaping the course of human life. Rather the power of culture has been usurped by the culture of power in almost every part of the world, greed and insecurity has led to consumerism and domination. What we have now is a culture of lies and death propelled by fear and profit. Humanity has turned anti-life. We are now evolving a culture that does not have humans and life at its center. And, as Ali Mazrui would say, the ancestors are angry.

Having experienced and witnessed the methods of hegemonic forces Paulo Freire reminds us that: "cultural invasion always involves a parochial view of reality and the imposition of one's world view upon another." It is not a coincidence, therefore, that all hegemonic powers would have at their heart a cultural project. Domination through culture is subtle but total, less expensive but potent. It slowly dehumanizes as the oppressed are made to believe that they cannot be makers of culture. The 2020 activists correctly observed that "if we do not make our own culture we can be owned even without knowing it."[5]

Politics of World View

> 'In this world I will always be on the side of the poor
> I will always be on the side of those who have nothing –
> Those to whom even the peace of having nothing is denied'
>
> —*Federico Garcia Lorca*

A people's world view do not just remain as ideas, perspectives, knowledge and values; they translate into real policies, systems of governance, patterns of organisation and interaction, models of institutions and methods of conducting the internal and external affairs of a nation. Indeed history provides the best example to help us understand how the worldview of a nation has shaped its response to the realities it confronts. For instance a nation's decision to either declare war or to make peace is often determined by the way it gives meaning to concepts such as 'security' and 'peace'.

However, because the earth is inhabited by so many cultures with different cultural beliefs and because every human life requires the same basic elements to survive and because the earth's natural resources are limited, there is an overwhelming temptation for one's world view to dominate and control others, which has led to the creation of a world view of domination and power.

Historically speaking, in the European worldview, all animals, and natural resources have been viewed as the 'property' of humans. Some seem to hold the view that certain people had the 'right' to take whatever they wanted. For instance: Spain, England, France and Portugal sailed around the earth and claimed land after land under the flag of their crowns. Most were looking for gold and gems to fund ongoing feuds and enrich royal coffers. In America during the 19th century, "Manifest Destiny" set the justification for 'takings' where it states that territorial expansion of the United States is not only inevitable but divinely ordained.

Under this belief, the indigenous people of the continent – the Native Americans – were not viewed as 'human', and therefore had no rights of any kind. In much of Europe and America, slavery was just business. Slaves were no more than 'property', a commodity to be used as one pleased. It was a male dominated world with a male 'world view' that held women in much the same light and justified it by stating that this was how things were meant to be. It was this world view that sustained systems, cultures and governments to impose its will, and 'take' whatever it pleased since these acts were all perceived as right and justifiable under one guise or the other.

Currently it is this same world view that enables the forces of globalism to carry out its agenda of consumerism and exploitation through multi-national corporations and global institutions with little regard and no respect for any life, and proceed to take resources under the guise that they are providing jobs for the unemployed and improving the quality of life for the poor and the oppressed. This is especially true in cases of undeveloped countries. However the reality being that it never trickles down to the poor and the rich get richer; the poor stay poor, or worse.

While European world view focused exclusively on domination, stratification of society, consumerism, retributive justice, defined boundaries, individual rights and individualism, indigenous peoples' worldviews were based on collective rights, inclusiveness, egalitarianism, overlapping spheres of boundaries, accommodating rights, respecting nature, restorative justice and partnership. I remember with clarity my conversation with a Navajo elder, who had told me, that "Columbus was lost at sea, we found him, invited him for a night and he has now lived with us for more than 500 years." I don't think I need to share what the dominant world view and interpretation of this historical experience is?

It is clear that humanity manifests richness of human cultures and world views, but it is also very real that hegemonic cultures and world views continue to work towards imposing their own to create a universalised world view through force, imposition, domination and manipulation. Therefore for the struggling people, it becomes an imperative necessity to ask, how can a woman living in a male-dominated cultural worldview realize herself and her human potential when she's seen only as property or a childbearing tool? How can people living in hopeless poverty find their way to the comforts allowed only by the chosen few? How can the children working dawn to dark every day by the time they can walk raise themselves out of this kind of human entrapment? How can the youth escape the cycle of prostitution and drug addiction while the privileged daily step over them? What will it take to liberate disappearing cultures and oppressed people? Is it possible to liberate our minds and our world views and relocate our world views, when human security is at the center once again?

The Caravan

> 'Brute force, no matter how strongly applied,
> can never subdue the basic human desire for freedom and dignity'
> —*The Dalai Lama*

Here I would like to share a story my friend Babu Ayindo from Kenya once shared with me. It is an intriguing story adapted from an Arabic fable that clearly projects the dilemmas a nation is faced with.

In this story, a caravan of culture is peacefully meandering towards its own destination under the stars of history. One night, a major interruption takes place. The caravan is overtaken and strangers use force to suppress it. The strangers divert the caravan from its original route, taking it into an alluring but alien destination. Many months later, under the inspiration of people seeking justice and peace, the original owners of the caravan seek to bring the caravan under indigenous control. The question arises whether the caravan should continue? The strangers have brought it some considerable distance from what seemed to be its natural route. Should the caravan continue in its path of diversion? Should it seek to discover the precise point at which it was hijacked and deflected, and from there once again seek its destiny? Or is it possible to locate to bearing from this point without necessarily going to its original point of diversion?

Using the metaphor of the caravan as a point of reference I would like to briefly examine the course of Naga world view. I do recognize that since the Nagas are a nation of many peoples, it will not be possible here to go into details, but based on the common history, common experience, common struggle and the common vision of the Nagas, I have tried to provide a perspective of how the world view has shaped the Continuity and Change of the Naga nation.

Prior to invasion of the Naga homeland and imposition of alien social, cultural, economic and political systems and institutions, when the Naga caravan was still peacefully meandering towards its own destination under the stars of history; the Naga people carried their daily affairs founded on a world view based on freedom, interdependence, interrelation and democratic values. The vision of the people was to continue the recognition and respect of self-determination so that the practical realisation of an egalitarian society was made possible. Captain Butler, the British anthropologist and soldier wrote in 1875 that the purest form of democracy exists among the Nagas.

Naga world view is founded on the celebration of life – all folk lore and legends are based on a relationship with nature, land, the earth and giving thanks to the Creator. Committing violent unprovoked acts contradicts their value system. Hands are never raised against unarmed individuals; and women and children are highly recognised for their honesty, simplicity, a relational pattern based on mutual respect and equality and a collective form of consensual decision-making process.

However after the Naga caravan was overcome by strangers from another caravan, the Naga way of life, their culture and hence their world views have undergone tremendous change. The suppression of the Naga caravan by way of force and imposition of alien systems have resulted in the militarisation of the Naga society. Alien systems have taken their toll on traditional Naga society, which has historically been community based. Military suppression and being in a state of perpetual political and armed conflict during the past half century have caused the erosion of traditional infrastructures that once were the core of the Naga society. The very right of assembly has been eliminated as defined by the Armed Forces Special Powers Act where a gathering of five or more persons can be declared an unlawful assembly. Peoples' relationships are under the scrutiny as opportunities to be together such as community meetings, feasting, and community work has broken down. Traditional decision-making practices have also become a casualty of militarisation. The closeness between individuals is rapidly disappearing, as opportunities to be together are limited, consequently the social fibre has become only a relic of the past.

All sectors of Naga society are affected and usurped by alien systems that have been imposed upon indigenous systems of the Nagas. These systems are generally hierarchical and gender imbalanced which is counter to more egalitarian oral traditions. The policies and practices of colonisation are insidious, dividing and ruling as they institutionalize violence throughout society. Instances of divide and rule as well as fragmentation of political identity create conditions instilling fear, suspicion, mistrust and hatred, ultimately creating the image of an enemy. Dehumanizing neighbours, community members and family begins to take place paving the way for violence, which can gain momentum and take a life of its own. Eventually during the course of events, basic human needs are neglected and human rights are summarily violated.

The alien systems that were imposed on Naga society included two significant developments: the categorisation and discrimination against so-called "minor and major tribes" described as either backward or developed; and the shift from selecting leadership by consensus to the ballot box where people are victimised by electoral politics (not in a democratic sense but in processes that sustain and reinforce violence). The electoral process became a cloaked isolating method of choosing leaders that separates Nagas from each other, where people cast their votes in exchange for jobs, security, etc. Nagas lose their collective power through a more individualistic democratic method of decision-making and are abused by the power of the ballot box.

The introduction of alien systems supplanting local norms is leading to other visible consequences in Naga society. Trauma, which Naga people have experienced and internalised during the past fifty plus years, is being expressed through other forms of violence as Nagas turn the pain inward and outward, hurting themselves and others. Family life was disrupted, extended family values were challenged or simply discarded and a new money economy now determined new gender roles and relationships. It goes without saying that all these changes were hardly advantageous to the women.

Another significant example of structural violence ushered in by alien systems is the institutionalisation of customary law. Customary law blankets all aspects of Naga existence defining the continuum of how one interacts and restores relationships with other human beings, the land and nature. It is a living and evolving system of norms and practices. Any process undertaken to codify customary law only strengthens the institutionalisation of structural violence, hence legitimizing the powers that further tighten their control over people through the use of force. The integrity of customary law as a vital tool within the polity of Naga life is being challenged. Hence, for customary law to reclaim and rediscover itself as a life giving democratic concept, its applicability and relevance must be rooted in today's aspirations based on values that embrace the richness of human life and cultures with dignity and respect at the core of its worldview.

These acts of violence against one another contradict the Naga way of life and have begun to erode the meaning and purpose of co-existence. The occupation of the Naga caravan by strangers has greatly affected the Naga worldview. Since the Nagas no longer have the decision making power and are unable to determine their own political future at this point of time, their ability and capacity to make adjustments to internal and external influences and the forces of globalisation on their own terms and needs have been greatly affected. Therefore the weakening of the Naga social and moral fibre has only created conditions that assist hegemonic forces to impose their worldviews and their knowledge system on the Nagas.

As a result the Naga society has become passive and has been reduced to being 'spectators' to change and the realities that surround their lives. Indeed, there is a great sense of inaction and unresponsiveness to the aspiration and needs of the people. The systematic processes of assimilation the Naga caravan have stripped away the humanity of the Nagas and have taken away their capacity to be makers of their own culture.

Our Hopes and Our Strengths for Transformation

> 'There's no turning back......We will win.
> We are winning because ours is a revolution of mind and heart'.
> —*Cesar Chavez*

As Babu and Aküm remind us that for people who have

endured colonialism and imperialism, questions regarding culture remain in mire. Not only do we tend to doubt our humanity but also our very capacity to "cultus." Responding to hegemonic forces indigenous people and those who have survived colonialism are struggling with questions to modernity. Can our traditions and cultures modernize? Should we surrender to globalism [that poses as modern culture]? Or, better still, is it possible to modernize without westernizing? Writing in 1972, the Guyanese historian Walter Rodney captured the impact of this historical struggle in his classic, *How Europe Underdeveloped Africa*. Central to Rodney's argument is that colonialism removed Africa [and third world] from history. Besides the material and psychological effects, Africa lost one fundamental element 'Power'. "Power," wrote Rodney, "is the ultimate determinant in human society, being basic to the relations within any group and between groups". And more importantly, "when one society finds itself forced to relinquish power entirely to another society that in itself is a form of underdevelopment".[6]

Have third and fourth world people become spectators of history? Are the violent conflicts we experience a symptom of our search to regain power? Will the breaking from the yoke of cultural captivity be the most significant step in regaining power? Is our own greed and brutality a search to regain power and negotiate with other forces of violence? But this may only be one side of the story.

If a people's capacity to regain power and be makers of history is disrespected, regimented or entirely replaced, then such a people lose enormous treasure and power – their identity and very capacity to be human, to be makers of culture. In our experience it limits indigenous people's capacity and space to function within their own paradigm(s) and to pursue and implement their own ways of human association, interaction and endeavour. They lose the power for human action for change. They cease to know who they are and who they are not. This leads to uprootedness from land and other spheres of life. The most obvious consequences are dependence on alien institutions and other external agencies and cultural and structural violence. Put differently, humans become predictable and dysfunctional. They become a gullible uniform mass.

Indigenous traditions and culture are resilient. The resilience may not be found in books or films. Like their religions, it is lived. In times of crisis one may capture the manifestations of its precepts. It is culture that enhances the capacity to confront the realities not by merely embracing it but by critically determining and modernizing traditions. It seeks to promote life on its own conditions and understanding. And things will get better when more third and fourth world and indigenous people overcome the definitions of culture that suffocate their capacity to transform their world according to their needs as their ancestors did. This, as Bantu Steve Biko put it, is the gift the world is waiting for from the oppressed people.

Globalism provides little or no space for indigenous cultures to make reflective adjustments matching the needs and challenges that emerge from new encounters. "The most potent weapon in the hands of the oppressor," Bantu Steve Biko wrote, "is the mind of the oppressed." The culture of global hegemony dehumanizes. At the heart of any force wishing to dominate others would always be a cultural project.

While we must accept that the technological gap is very wide, we must overcome the superstition that technological advancement is equal to modernity. There is need to stop being fatalistic about the seemingly enormous advancement in science and technology. We must accept that modernity is not just about historical time and technology but the quality and character of the lives we lead. And if other manifestations, besides the economic were to be used to judge whether we are modern or not, then we, the people living in the globalised 21st century would rank poorly. Perhaps worse than our ancestors who lived in caves. Listen to Boal:

> Many people, who in the past used to defend the poor, today affirm that globalisation is inevitable and modern. They forget that all hegemonic powers have always been globalizing and that to globalize is in their nature. From Pax Romana on, or the Incas and the Aztecs or the British and American Empires, or Hitler's Thousand-year Reich, imperialism has always sought to monopolize the world. There is nothing modern about the modern world; they are still troglodytes.[7]

Can our traditions modernize? We should echo the words of Luigi Guissani that traditions are not handed over to us so that we become fossilised within them. Like our ancestors, we should be able to develop tradition, "even to the point of profoundly changing it." However, in order to develop the capacity to transform tradition we must "act with" what our ancestors gave us. This means using tradition critically, filtering it through our own praxis. However, "using tradition critically does not mean doubting its value – even if this is what is suggested by the current mentality."[8]

Ironically, the more we run away from our traditions and seek to modernize within the precepts of other people's cultures, the more we become "fossilised." We must identify and reject the history that sought to portray us as non-humans. At the same time we must trust our true history, experience and capacity to transform. We must begin by asserting that all people, in the attempt to come to terms with fellow humans, nature and the supernatural, encounter conflicts. In responding to these conflicts and challenges, values are evolved and culture is created. Ideally, any people become makers of history in an ever-continuing negotiation with these basic elements.

It is critical to recognize that the freedom and justice of humankind is tied with one another. Ideally we should be living in an interdependent, interconnected and interrelated circle of life. Problem is that a few people would like to dominate the circle. And we are against that.

The Naga struggle is an expression of its history as free people and hence derives its strength from its world view which is founded on freedom and self determination so that the Nagas themselves are guided by a vision of democracy, justice and peace. Nagas want a culture that is life giving, supporting and meets their needs. Simply put, the Naga caravan is seeking to bring the Naga caravan under its indigenous control, so that they may reclaim their humanity and dignity and once again discover their gift to become makers of their own culture by liberating their minds and their human spirit and enriching their worldviews based on their experiences.

And as some people of great faith have said, "The dog barks, but the caravan continues...."

REFERENCES

1. Steve Biko, 1997, *I Write What I Like*. London: Bowearden, p 96.
2. G.Bennars and R.Njoroje, 1996, *Philosophy and Education in Africa*. Nairobi: PanAfrica Press. Emphasis added. See also Babu Ayinda, Sam Doe and Jan Jenner, *When You are the Peacebuilder*. Washington Dc: United States Institute of Peace, 2001.
3. The 2020 papers, *Derry Frontline: Culture and Education*, 1994.
4. *Augusto Boal, Legislative Theatre*. New York: Routledge, 1998. p. 178
5. The 2020 papers. p. 7
6. Walter Rodney, 1972, *How Europe Underdeveloped Africa*. Nairobi: Heinemann, p. 245, Emphasis added.
7. *Legislative Theatre*, p. 36
8. Luigi Guissani, 1997, *The Religious Sense*, Montreal: Mc Gill University, p. 38.

Contributors

A. K. Ray, (IFS Retired) Executive Council Member, MAKAIAS

D. N. Venuh, Reader and Head, Department of History and Archaeology, Nagaland University, Kohima.

Dr. S. V. Babu, Senior Lecturer, Department of History and Archaeology, Nagaland University, Kohima.

Kekhrie Yhome, Research scholar, J. N. U, New Delhi.

Akum Longchari, Research scholar.

D. Koulie, Senior Lecturer and Head in-charge, Department of Tenyidie, Nagaland University, Kohima.

Akang Ao, Principal, Kohima Law College, Kohima.

J. Longkumer, Senior Lecturer, Department of Extension, Nagaland University, Medziphema campus, Dimapur.

Charles Chasie, Senior journalist and writer and also author of the book "Naga Imbroglio".

Anungla Aier, Reader and Head, Department of Anthropology, Kohima Science College, Jotsoma.

Prof. Lanunungsang, Dean of Social Science, Department of Sociology, Nagaland University, Lumami campus.

Index